MW00653126

The Way I
The North Dakota Frontier Experience
Book Three: The Cowboys and Ranchers

The Way It Was

The North Dakota Frontier Experience
Book Three:

The Cowboys
& Ranchers

Everett C. Albers and D. Jerome Tweton, Editors

THE GRASS ROOTS PRESS
Fessenden, North Dakota 58438
2004

This book is dedicated to the old cowboys and ranchers who told their stories so well about seventy years ago. The series is dedicated to the memory of North Dakota pioneers.

Editors: *Everett C. Albers and D. Jerome Tweton*
Designer: *Otto Design of Bismarck, ND*

© 1999 by The Grass Roots Press
PO Box 407
Fessenden, North Dakota 58438-0407

Copyright is claimed in the Prefaces; Introductions to the Interviews collected by the Works Progress Administration in cooperation with the State Historical Society of North Dakota; Index; and editing of the original interviews which are in the public domain. All rights reserved to the material for which copyright is claimed.

Published by The Grass Roots Press

Printed in Canada

10 9 8 7 6 5 4 3 2

International Standard Book Number: 0-9650778-7-3 (Book 3)
International Standard Book Number: 0-9650778-1-0 (6 Volume Set)

Library of Congress Control Number: 98-89183

Table of Contents

Acknowledgments

*T*HE COVER PHOTOGRAPH and those on pages 34 and 37 come from the Fred Hultstrand History in Pictures Collection, NDIRS-NDSU, Fargo. The hand-colored picture is of "a herd of wild bronchos brought in from Montana — about 1900." All other photographs are from the collection of the State Historical Society of North Dakota. The Grass Roots Press gratefully acknowledges the support of the staff of the Society, particularly the folks in the Society's archives and library, and especially Todd Strand who serves as curator of the photo collection. The State Historical Society of North Dakota is the home of 5,000 stories of North Dakota pioneers from which we gleaned the dozen in this volume, several of which came from a special Works Progress Administration project which involved collecting first-person stories from the oldest ranchers in the state.

We editors thank our wives, Leslie Albers and Paula Tweton. They have proofread, given advice, and supported this ongoing project with the kind of good-humored notion that work should be fun that Margaret Barr Roberts brought to ranch work in the early days in the Dakota Badlands.

About the editing . . .

The words are those of the early cowboys and ranchers. We changed some of the stories recorded in the third-person by WPA workers to first-person narratives. We also made some punctuation and grammatical changes and occasionally inserted words for clarity.

D. Jerome Tweton

From the Old West to the New West

D. Jerome Tweton

From 1881 through 1885 the Little Missouri and Missouri Plateau regions boomed.

In McKenzie County between 1900 and 1904 so many small ranchers came in that they were able to drive off the big outfits.

The role of the traditional cowboy diminished.

IN 1879 UNDER HEADLINES such as "The Promised Land" and "Fortunes to be Made" the *Bismarck Tribune* exuberantly proclaimed that western North Dakota possessed "the best grazing lands in the world" and that in the Badlands "grass . . . is breast high to the horses." Three years later, after the Northern Pacific had laid its tracks through the Badlands, the *Dickinson Press* pictured the region as a land of milk and money where even "mothers-in-law forget to scold." The newspaper went on to explain that in the Badlands "is found the best grasses, water, and shelter." A writer for the faraway *New York Times* warned its readers to be cautious about the boastings of

Dakota newspapers but concluded: "Still, I believe the subject has not been overstated."

"Authorities" on the Great Plains and its potential as a profitable place to raise cattle agreed with the newspaper assessments. Dr. Hiram Latham, a surgeon with the Union army during the Civil War, in his book *Trans-Missouri Stock Raising*, praised the high plains and the cattle business in glowing terms. He even started up a ranch in Wyoming. Robert Strahorn, a journalist with General Crook in 1876, wrote three handbooks on the high plains in the late 1870s. He demonstrated that investment in cattle was sound and fantastically profitable — 25 to 60 percent per annum.

No one stirred the imagination or ignited cattle fever more than General James S. Brisbin. His *The Beef Bonanza or How to Get Rich on the Plains*, which appeared in 1881, dazzled the imaginations of potential cattle investors. Brisbin, who spent twelve years at western forts, observed: "To me the West is a never ceasing source of wonder and I cannot imagine why people remain in the overcrowded East, while so many lands and chances are to the west of them." Under chapter titles such as "The Money to be Made" and "Millions in Beef," he presented statistics that documented cattle profits at between 20 and 40 percent. An investment of $250,000 would reach $810,000 within five years, according to Brisbin.

These optimistic reports were reaching the public just as the cattle raisers' last frontier was opening up in Dakota west of the Missouri, especially in Little Missouri country. Unlike the farmers' frontier which moved east to west, the cattle frontier moved from south to north. The demand for beef during the Civil War stimulated the expansion of the range industry in Texas. In the 1870s the frontier moved northward along the western Great Plains as eastern and European capital flowed west in great gushes. The Colorado range increased from 70,000 to 800,000 head and Wyoming from 11,000 to 500,000 during the 1870s. By 1880 over 4,000,000 Texas cattle had been driven to the northern and high plains.

And cattle raising became highly organized, big business. The Consolidated Land, Cattle Raising and Wool Growing Corporation capitalized at $10,000,000. Hundreds of smaller corporations, many managed out of London and Edinburgh, sprang up as cattle fever reached high intensity. In 1882 and 1883 over two hundred new cattle companies were incorporated.

By 1880 the beef bonanza was taking its toll on the rich grasses of Colorado and Wyoming, and cattle companies were beginning to look northward for new places on the government's free-use open range. Between 1880 and 1884 over 500,000 head were moved into the Black Hills region of southwestern Dakota Territory.

The northward thrust of herds and the investor's constant search for better grass led to the opening of the cattle kingdom's last frontier — the Little Missouri country of northern Dakota, the Badlands. The area offered the three essential ingredients for ranching: shelter, grass, and water. And the east-west rails of the Northern Pacific cut through the territory by 1881.

Badlands Cowboys About 1888
A.C. Huidekoper is seated third from the left.

Among the first to recognize the merits of the Badlands as cattle country were A.C. Huidekoper of Meadville, Pennsylvania; W.E. Hughes of Dallas, Texas; and two Minnesotans, H.B. Wadsworth and W.L. Hawley. In 1881 Huidekoper met Howard and Eldon Eaton of Pittsburgh while buffalo hunting in western North Dakota. The three formed the Custer Trail Cattle Company. The Eatons managed; Huidekoper provided the capital. Unlike most outfits, the company purchased a private range of 23,000 acres of railroad land between Deep and Davis creeks where it ran about a thousand head. Shortly after the Eatons and Huidekoper launched their effort, the Continental Land and Cattle Company, capitalized at $3,000,000 and headed by

W.E. Hughes of Dallas, began operations between Box Elder and Little Beaver creeks. Its herd at times surpassed 60,000. The Bad Lands Cattle Company, organized by Wadsworth and Hawley, developed its ranching enterprise on the Little Missouri near the mouth of the Little Cannonball. The big Texas outfits drove their cattle into the area from southern ranges during the summer. The OX ran over 15,000 and the Three Sevens nearly 10,000. Clearly, by 1883, the Badlands and the country west of the Missouri were becoming Dakota's cattle kingdom.

That year brought the nation's attention to the region when four highly visible persons caught Little Missouri cattle fever. Pierre Wibaux, twenty-five-year-old son of a French textile manufacturer, refused to follow in his father's footsteps, studied the cattle business in Chicago, and with $10,000 provided by his not-too-happy papa, struck out for the Little Missouri. He selected a range site on Beaver Creek and began what proved to be a successful operation.

Another twenty-five-year-old by the name of Theodore Roosevelt, a New York lawmaker and Harvard graduate, also viewed the Badlands as a land of opportunity. Although he came to hunt buffalo, he ended up in the cattle business. He bought out Wadsworth and Hawley, and with Sylvane Ferris and A.W. Merrifield as managers, Roosevelt took over the Maltese Cross Ranch to the south of Little Missouri. Later he established the Elkhorn Ranch, almost 40 miles to the north. In all, Roosevelt invested about $80,000 in his cattle venture.

Still a third twenty-five-year-old decided upon the Little Missouri country as a place, in this case, to become (in his words), "the richest financier in the world." Antoine-Amédée-Marie-Vincent-Amat Manca Vallombrosa, the Marquis de Morès, was his name and meat packing was his game. The French nobleman's plan was to dress the cattle right in the midst of the cattle range and ship the beef via refrigerator car to markets in the East. By the end of the year his plan and his plant were in operation. And, his town of Medora was booming.

Sir John Pender was far from being twenty-five years old. But he was indeed very rich. An internationally known and respected London financier, Sir John had financed the laying of the Atlantic cable and now desired to increase his wealth through cattle ranching. He along with two New York City tycoons, Henry Gorringe and Abram Hewitt,

The Marquis de Morès prepares for a hunt
The Marquis is standing center. His wife Medora is seated side-saddle.

organized the Little Missouri Land and Stock Company. Pender hired
Gregor Lang, who knew more about cattle than most of the Badlands
ranchers, to manage his business.

From 1881 through 1885 the Little Missouri and the Missouri Plateau regions boomed. Brisbin and the other "experts" had been correct
— good money could be made in cattle. Then, it all fell apart. The
drought summer of 1886 cut an already scanty supply of grass. The winter of 1886-1887 came early and stayed late. An endless barrage of blizzards, accompanied by terrible cold, spelled disaster for the northern
range cattle industry. About 75 percent of the cattle perished. "The
losses are crippling," lamented Roosevelt. Many quit; some scaled
back; some reorganized.

The large Texas outfits reduced their operations, but continued to
graze their summer herds in Dakota into the 1890s. Failing in business,
the Marquis de Morès went back to France. Roosevelt swallowed his
pride and his losses and entered fully into eastern politics. Wibaux and
Huidekoper reorganized and continued to ranch with success.

But, the days of the big range ranchers were numbered. Small
ranchers, such as those who appear in this book, began to take over. For
example, in McKenzie County between 1900 and 1904, so many small
ranchers came in that they were able to drive off the large-scale range
operations of the big outfits. The terrible winter of 1896-1897 had al-

D. Jerome Tweton

ready pushed many big ranchers to the south. Then, too, the second boom homesteaders began to carve out farms in the middle of what had been free range country.

The last of the big ranchers to go was Huidekoper and his HT Ranch. In 1905 he sold his 63,446 acres of range and disposed of his stock. The day of the large bonanza ranch was over.

The heyday, the golden years, of the range cattle industry ran from the 1870s into the 1890s. The cattle enterprises could not have been successful without a large and cheap labor force — the cowboys. They were young, hardworking, and poorly paid. The movies with stars such as John Wayne, Alan Ladd, Roy Rogers, Tom Mix or Gene Autry and popular fiction with writers such as Owen Wister and Zane Grey have romanticized the life and times of the American cowboy. There was not much romance in a sixteen-hour day; in driving cattle along dusty trails or through heat, rain, cold, or snow; or in sharing a bug-infested bunk-house with a bunch of other cowboys. The life of the cowboy was tough, but without the cowboy, the cattle industry could not have survived and been profitable. Most cowboys stayed in the saddle for five or six years. Then, they opted for a less strenuous and more rewarding life in a western town.

How many cowboys were there during the golden years of the range cattle industry? We don't know. We have better counts on the number of cattle. That in and of itself tells us something about how the big outfits regarded the cowboy — necessary cogs in the machinery of a large company.

With the passing of the large outfits and the coming of the small ranchers into western North Dakota, the role of the traditional cowboy diminished. Small ranchers looked at themselves as rancher-cowboys and did most of the ranch work themselves with the help of family members. To be sure, many small ranchers employed a cowboy or two or three — even more on a seasonal basis — but their number decreased substantially after 1900. The Old West was now the New West.

The Right Stuff Needed to Make It on the Dakota Range

Everett C. Albers

They danced in tune with the wild country their rambling, gambling approach to life dictated, a thirst for the freedom of the wide-open spaces that brought them to western Dakota in the first place.

They want the world to know that the dozen or so years back then were the best any freedom-loving American could ever hope to live.

CHARLIE COLGROVE COULD BE SPEAKING for most who came to western Dakota to ranch or work for ranchers: "This God-dang country suits me," he says. Charlie is given to a bit of mild cussing, and he is as cussedly crusty as any who came out to the last of the open ranges to make some money and have a good time. It was indeed a land of "milk and money," a place where there were buffalo bones lying all over the place — an easy source of ready cash.

Wagonloads of buffalo bones lined up in Minot in 1888

Game was so plentiful, so easy to get, that Rueben Humes recalls thousands of grouse and hundreds of antelope ready for the taking. Humes says that "the grouse would light in the cottonwood tree. I shot the grouse that were on the lower branches and worked up. I shot the grouse in the head, and as long as they tumbled to the ground, the other grouse would not fly away, but if I just wounded one and it flew away, the others would usually follow. In half an hour or so more chickens would light in the tree. Some mornings I would kill as high as 50 chickens. I kept a few and sold the others for 15 cents each in Dickinson. They were packed and shipped east." The country was so wild that Mae Caldwell Moran says, "It was nothing to see a cinnamon [brown] bear in a herd. They never did much harm and would walk along with a herd." T. B. Knight calls western North Dakota "a hunter's paradise." Young John Inkster remembers "fish so thick in the Mouse River that we could shovel them out with pitch forks. I remember that when I was twelve or thirteen I speared a pickerel that weighed 35½ pounds. It was so strong that it nearly ran off with me." C.O. Armstrong and his friend Ed killed a bear after it destroyed a steer. Ed tried a taste of the bear's heart —

"God, it's like chewing rubber," he said. Rueben Humes recalls gray and buffalo wolves killing cattle and horses, bobcats getting to the sheep, and coyotes, like many of the hunters, killing whatever they could, far in excess of what they could eat.

In many other ways, no few of those who came and stayed on in western North Dakota were like the coyote they disliked so intensely — tough, resilient, adaptable, wily, and playful. They came not only for the money to be made in ranching — or to be had for picking buffalo bones off the ground or grouse off the cottonwoods. "There were no such things as fences in those days. Nobody owned land. You would have been insulted if anybody offered you a piece of land as a gift. You didn't want a piece. You felt that you owned all there was," says Margaret Barr Roberts. As English-born Thomas Jefferson (curiously, his best buddy in his Canadian railroad days was George Washington) concludes, "When I first came to the United States, the first thing I noticed was the freedom everyone was enjoying. It seemed that everyone had a chance to work at whatever he wanted, and he was able to get ahead." The fences came, of course — with the homesteaders and their claims to small plots of the vast grasslands. Laments Charlie Colgrove, "we got closed out on ranching in 1906 because the damn farmers came in and run us out." Charlie says that he "followed the ranching game till the farmers got too damn thick." T.B. Knight agrees: "When the farmers began to come here in large numbers, things changed, and not for the better." Knight takes to farming himself — in self defense and adaptable self confidence: "I thought that if all these farmers could make a go of it at farming, so could I." But, Knight ruminated, "I thought of what the Indians said: leave the land right-side-up or famine will result."

Famine in the land of "milk and money" was the least of possibilities in the early years on the western Dakota frontier. There was plenty of trouble, however, in a place better suited for coyotes than all but the hardiest. Raging blizzards, killing snows which came as early as September, wiped out herds and marked those who braved nature's fury with the scars of the frostbitten. Caught with his friend Ed in a blizzard while herding sheep, Rueben Humes records the aftermath: "Our flesh turned purple. . . . Ed came back from the hospital in twenty days. He did not look like the same person at all. His face was sunk in and full of holes. On my face and body were about twenty spots covered with proud flesh where I had been frozen. These places would not heal so I was taken to Dickinson and put in the hospital. This was the end of sheep herding for me." Thomas Jefferson remembers September 1900 as "the worst blizzard I know of, and the cattle were ranging on the prairie when the blizzard was raging its worst. After the storm had abated we found that there were only three of the 300 head left. The others had mired down in a creek." The man Jefferson worked for lost Black Angus he had just purchased for $100 each. Charlie Colgrove says, "I'll never forget it, old '86 — the Hash-Knife outfit lost 500 head. There was just one damn blizzard after another."

By 1900, much of the game and all of the buffalo were gone. The Indians of North Dakota were on reservations facing the kind of famine that seemed impossible a short decade earlier. Thomas Jefferson says that following the September blizzard, "These cattle . . . were pulled from the creek by the Indians who took them to their camp and ate them. When the Long X lost all its cattle the Indians also cleaned them up for the ranch." To some, Indians were like the ravishing wolves, rattlesnakes, and steer-killing bear — that part of the West that had to be tamed. Caroline Elizabeth Fay as a youngster saw "Many Indians with their squeaking carts drawn by little Indian ponies passed by our door on the Old Fort Totten Trail. I had heard many stories about the Indians. The first time they passed our house, the wheels of their carts were stained crimson to the hubs from the crushed wild strawberries along the trail. I was almost paralyzed with fear. I thought it was blood." She goes on to say, "Our friend in the East offered to send firearms for our protection, for the papers were full of hair-raising tales of the savages in the West. However, they never harmed us." Mae Caldwell Moran says, "There weren't any neighbors for six or seven years after we settled in the country. There were lots of Indians, but they were friendly, and we liked them. Those Indians and the fellows that worked for us and the folks at home were about all the folks we saw from end of one year till the next." Mary E. Ross Coulter remembers that "while they were the cause of many anxious days and nights, no harm ever came to us from them. They were always allowed to take what food they wanted whenever they came. Mother felt the Indians were quite considerate because they took only about one-half of whatever food they found."

The real threat to survival was not neighboring Indians but the weather and a perennial menace, the prairie fire. John Inkster says that one had cowboys working "until we couldn't breathe, but we kept the fire from getting into the timber. That was about 1900. I remember that after the fire was out, we lay on the ground and panted for an hour." Mae Caldwell Moran and her brother Jay fought one for days: "Pa killed a steer, tied ropes to each end, and then tied the rope to our saddle horns and had us drag it back and forth through the fire. After that fire, you would not have known I was a white girl. The smoke and fire had burnt right into my skin. It took two months it get it off, before I looked like a white person again. Some of the fire fighters were overcome, as it was hard to get food to us, and none of us had too much water. I remember that for two days I only had one piece of bread for food, but Jay and I did have a water sack that held out for two days."

It took cooperation to make it out there, back in those days. Perhaps that is why folks trusted each other so much. They needed each other at roundups and during prairie fires. In a place so sparsely populated, they depended on each other for that critical need of all humans, the company of each other. They would travel up to 100 miles to go to a dance in the dead of winter when they knew they might be risking their lives. Perhaps the most telling tale of how much a lonesome cowboy or rancher missed good company is the story told by "Doc" Spry about Abe Owens, the cowpuncher who rode 100 miles and spent more than a week to take a visiting lady across the Badlands to a dance in Wibaux, Montana. He arranges for a chaperone, hires a buggy, and on the way back goes 20 or more miles out of the way several times to show off his date at ranches — despite her great discomfort because she can hardly walk after riding more than 20 miles on a lark and suffering infected legs as a result. Concludes Spry, "As near as I could figure it, Owens was nine days and traveled 300 miles to take the romantic girl to a dance." John Inkster remembers the first girl he danced with. C.O. Armstrong relates a story about cowpunchers descending on a dance hall: "All of the girls had on cowpunchers' hats. In those days they danced the old fashioned way, dancing one way and then reversing, and the cowpunchers would shoot every time they would reverse, and they weren't very particular where they shot. The fiddlers were getting rather scared, so they dropped their fiddles and went out the window. We had some pretty good fiddlers in the bunch, so two of the cowboys picked up the fiddles and started to play, and the dance went on."

They danced in tune with the wild country their rambling, gambling approach to life dictated, a thirst for the freedom of the wide-open spaces that brought them to western Dakota in the first place. They talk about having fun. As Margaret Barr Roberts says, "I was full of the old Nick myself in those days, always ready for a joke." With the help of Teddy Roosevelt and another friend, she pays back the self-righteous wife of Deacon Cummins who transgresses the unwritten law of western hospitality by putting down the group who dared come visiting on a Sunday. They return later on a Sunday and convince Mrs. Cummins, who is working in her garden, that the day is the Sabbath, for they are dressed in their finest clothes. The elaborate pranks included putting on a show for the new homesteaders, as Thomas Jefferson remembers: "If we knew a party [of settlers] was coming in . . . , we would put on some act to welcome them. Sometimes we would get a horse that would buck, and when the stage come in sight of the business district, we made him buck and cause a ruckus to impress the settlers. It was also common for us to get four or five men to shoot off their revolvers while riding their horses through the street at full gallop, just for the effect."

They gambled — big time in the case of the ranchers who risked the modern equivalent of millions to buy cattle they lost so quickly in blizzards. There were those who preferred a poker game to anything else, as stagecoach driver Pebbles, who, Thomas Jefferson says, "found that he had lost the mail sack. Instead of going back himself, he hired a man to find the sack and bring it to Williston. He would rather play poker." The cowboys would often spend everything they earned in a year in a single day of fun. Rueben Humes recalls, "After we had loaded the cattle in freight cars in Dickinson, the men were paid off. They proceeded at once to get drunk in the blind pigs. They had a noisy good time. Some took part in poker games. We spent one day in Dickinson loafing. Morse then told the men to be ready to leave the next morning. By this time most of the men were broke. We made the return trip in three

Taking time for a card game on the range

days." John Inkster says, "There was much drinking, gambling, and wild parties" at the ranch of Coutts Majorbanks, who "was Lord Thursby, a very hard drinker who was shipped out to Dakota to get him away from the family so he would not disgrace the titled English family. He had hounds for fox hunting, but there were no fox, and he couldn't catch the coyotes, although he tried. One day he became angry at his hounds because they were so useless that he went out and killed them all." And Charlie Colgrove tells the story of a man who "brought a load of hay to Dickinson on a wagon hitched to two old nags. That same day the Hash-Knife outfit was in here drinking and shooting up the town, and old Taminlin got right on a street corner when the Hash-Knifers took a few pops at him. Taminlin seemed to go right down in the hay, and one horse was killed. After the shooting let up, old Taminlin crawled out and said, 'Well, why didn't they get old Ted, too?' He got a good horse from the Hash-Knife outfit for the one they killed. That outfit would raise hell and tear things galley-west, then pay back for any damage they had done to anyone. They were pretty good that way."

Finally, the first who came to western Dakota were good at telling stories. Maybe it was those long winter nights, or perhaps the fourteen hours alone in the saddle that gave birth to mostly true tales of the way it was. From C.O. Armstrong's poems to the picturesque portraits that

Charlie Colgrove spins punctuated with "Holy God!" the dozen recollections in this book are the stuff of master storytellers. The reader will not soon forget Armstrong's recounting of that night in the dance hall, Colgrove's tale of Taminlin, Caroline Elizabeth Fay's memory of the blizzard of 1892, Humes' trip to find a homestead for three drunken Finlanders, John Inkster's encounter with the vigilantes, Thomas Jefferson's portrait of the poker-loving Mr. Pebbles, T.B. Knight's tale of Bill Stroud's trip to town for chawing tobacco, Mae Caldwell Moran's story of fighting the prairie fire, Margaret Barr Roberts' delightful account of giving Mrs. Cummins her comeuppance with Teddy Roosevelt, Mary E. Ross Coulter's description of her sheriff-father's prisoners, "Doc" Spry's unforgettable story of Abe Owen's date, or Alfred White's description of what happened to Peter Molloy, notorious for giving his hotel patrons dirty towels.

What's most remarkable in all their tales is what they don't say. There's not much complaining and no regrets about choosing to come and stay on the western Dakota grasslands. To be sure, they hated to see the homesteaders come in, the fences go up, the counties organized, and the last frontier of open-range grasslands turned over by the plow. But they want the world to know that the dozen or so years back then were the best any freedom-loving American could ever hope to live. Were they gathered around during a dance listening to Charlie Colgrove, they would probably shoot off a round to the ceiling in an "Amen!" to his "This God-dang country suits me." They suited the country with the right stuff, or they never would have been around to tell their stories.

In The Badlands: Hunter, Rancher, Cowboy Poet

C.O. Armstrong

Thank you friend —
now lay me down.
Bury me not near a town
Dig my grave on the divide
That the trail crosses,
where we used to ride . . .

At age seven C.O. Armstrong came to Dakota Territory with his parents when his father, James Armstrong, was ordered to Fort Totten in 1869. The senior Armstrong had emerged from the Civil War as an officer with Company F of the 17th Infantry. Young Armstrong learned "Indian language" at the fort, and when he was twelve years old, he became a government messenger. Several years later he carried the mail between Fort Lincoln and Fort Keogh. He hunted in the Badlands and worked for Pierre Wibaux and took part in the roundup with Theodore Roosevelt. A poet, he published often in newspapers in western North Dakota. In 1887 he "went to ranching for himself." He married Elsie Rowe at the Kidder Hotel in Dickinson in 1900 and in 1910 homesteaded near Fairfield.

The Cowboy's Last Request

My dear true friend come by me sit,
And what I say, please don't forget.
Take my saddle, rope and bed
Do them up when I am dead.
Send them to my only brother
Tell him that I'm joining mother.
And to you I leave my gun
Not because of what you've done.
For that's a debt I could not pay
As you cared for me night and day.
You gave me water, bathed my head,
You held me gently, smoothed my bed
You brought me food which was so good —
I could not eat, try as I would.
The little horse I used to ride
I leave to one to have been my bride.
She's at the ranch, just over the hill,
Tell her we'll meet should it be God's will.
And to the one my horse I gave
May she sometime ride to my grave
My body deep in the ground will be
My soul and spirit shall always see
Her — when she comes and when she goes,
I know she'll have that faded rose,
The one I plucked for her in June,
Not thinking then we'd part so soon.
What is the use? — God's will must be.
Please raise my head so that I can see
Across the yard to the corral.
Oh, there are the horses I love so well.
Thank you friend — now lay me down.
Bury me not near a town
Dig my grave on the divide
That the trail crosses, where we used to ride,
Where from the ranch my grave she'll see

Then she will sometimes think of me.
I thank you now for all you've done,
My life must go with the setting sun.
Arrange it so I face the West.
Please raise my head and take my hand.
I see you now as there you stand
Strong and well, but I must go
To the long, long home that no one knows.

* * * * * * * * * *

ON THE W-BAR RANCH on the Little Missouri, owned by the French aristocrat, Pierre Wibaux, many interesting events took place. The one I am about to tell is about our beloved doctor, Dr. Stickney, whose home was in Dickinson, North Dakota. The cowboys had brought in a bunch of horses and were working them in the corral, when in some way Sid Tarbell fell and broke his arm. Dr. Stickney was called, and he started on his long journey from Dickinson, a distance of about 100 miles, on horseback. In those days every one was ready to do what they could, so the doctor would ride his horse until it was tired, then he would borrow another and he would ride on. On this occasion I happened to be one of the men who had loaned him a horse. When he came to the river, it was a roaring torrent, and the only way he could get there was by swimming, so he swam his horse across the river. When he arrived at the W-Bar Ranch, it was too late; his patient was very low, as gangrene had set in. When he looked at him, he knew that his time here was very short, but he did what he could for him, staying until he was buried. They made a coffin of boards and buried him on the W-Bar Ranch. He was not only a doctor but a friend in need to these pioneer people, and they all loved him. There is a beautiful butte near the ranch and Dr. Stickney always admired it whenever he was out there. Herds of black tailed deer roamed over this butte. This butte is known as Stickney Butte.

Ed Meyers and myself were camped on the Magpie Creek. I had come up to the ranch after supplies, and while I was gone he went after a deer, but run on to a bear. When I returned the next morning, he told me he had run on to a bear track. So we followed the trail and came to a big bunch of green cedars. The bear had got in a fight with a three-year-old steer in this thicket, and when she had hit at the steer and missed him, she tore big pieces of bark off the trees. She killed the steer, ate about 50 or 75 pounds, and wandered on. We followed her trail, and when she went in the den, we tried to smoke her out, but she didn't come out. High up over the den were huge petrified stumps, so I told Ed to go up and roll them down, and I would watch at the mouth of the den and shoot her, if she came out. Ed stopped up the mouth of the den with stumps and was going after her the next morning. About 100 yards above the mouth of the den was a small hole; smoke was coming out here, so we went to examine it to see if she could dig out. So we stopped that up. Ed wanted to clean his gun. He had a gun string with a rag on it and he drawed it about half way down through the gun barrel, and he broke the string, leaving the gun plugged up. I told him while he was monkeying around, I would go down to the mouth of the den to see if everything was all right. When I got in 50 feet of the den, I heard a noise down there. The bear was throwing these huge stumps out of the den, the same as a boy would throw marbles. The bear started right after me. I shot her in the shoulder and broke her shoulder joint. Then she started the other way, and I shot her five more times before she fell; she was lying there apparently dead. I leaned my gun against a tree, knelt down and was going to take hold of her, and noticed her roll her eye a little bit, so I shot her again in the head. She was just playing possum. The next morning we went out with a sled and hauled her in to camp. Ed hauled the hindquarters into Dickinson and sold them to Joe Green. The funny part was Ed had never eaten any bear meat, so he wanted to cut a piece and cook it. I told him it would be so strong he couldn't eat it, and he said he would take the heart anyway. He sat up half the night boiling the heart, and after he got it cooked, he started to eat it, so I said, "Ed, how do you like bear heart," and he said, "God, it's like chewing rubber."

During the hard winter of 1886 more than 1,000 head of cattle died; it was reported a 40 percent loss but it was an 80 percent loss. The cattlemen thought all of the cattle could not have died but had drifted on to the reservation. Four outfits, Maltese Cross (Roosevelt's outfit), No.

37, Hatchet Knife, and the Henry Boise all started out together to the Cannonball River, where it emptied into the Big Missouri River. Roosevelt's outfit worked up as far as Mandan, and Hatchet Knife worked down as far as the Standing Rock Reservation. The town of Winona was just across the river from Fort Yates. Two boys left the outfit and rode ahead into Winona, and the next day the whole outfit pulled into Fort Yates. These two boys on the other side said, "When you had all made camp to come over." As we couldn't cross the river on our horses, we had to cross on a skiff. Winona was noted for her dance hall girls, and they called themselves "fairies." We were met on the other side by our two boy friends and one girl they called "Goldie." This girl had one of the cowboy's hats on, and the cowboy had on her stockings and hat on with the stockings on the outside of his pants. One of the largest buildings in town was the saloon; the back part was used for a dance hall. The citizens of the town hadn't used these two boys very well when they were there alone. So these boys told about the treatment they got. Then the boys commenced to shoot up the town and they shot it up good and plenty. The girls who worked in the hotel were so scared they went to their rooms and stayed there. So we couldn't get anything to eat there very handy. There was an old Irish lady who opened up her home and fed us. When we went to her house, she said that she would see that we got plenty to eat if we wouldn't shoot. The boys were pretty full [drunk]; we had hard-boiled eggs for supper, and one of the boys wouldn't sit at the table. Riley sat up on the sideboard and put his feet on the table; he was so drunk that he was eating eggs, shell and all, and Bill said, "How do you like that hen fruit." Riley said, "It's pretty good but the skins are pretty tough." We asked the old lady how much we owed her, and she said that she had never done that kind of business and didn't know what it was worth. So we gave her a dollar apiece and went over town. About the only place of amusement was the dance hall, so we went there to spend the evening. There were two fiddlers playing for the dance; the window was up and the musicians were sitting by the window. All of the girls had on cowpunchers' hats. In those days they danced the old fashioned way, dancing one way and then reversing, and the cowpunchers would shoot every time they would reverse, and they weren't very particular where they shot. The fiddlers were getting rather scared, so they dropped their fiddles and went out the window. We had some pretty good fiddlers in the bunch, so two of the cowboys picked up the fiddles and started to play, and the dance went on. We were getting hungry, as it was after midnight, so we went up to the old lady's house, and she had gone to bed. Bill pounded on the door until she came down and opened it for us and asked her if she would get us something to eat and she said if we wouldn't shoot. So Bill told her we wouldn't. The boys had taken their girl fairies with them. The old lady did not care to feed the girls as she did not approve of the way they acted. Then the boys told her that if the girls couldn't, they wouldn't either, so she gave her consent and fed them all. About two o'clock in the morning we all went back to the saloon. Up to this time the sheriff had never shown up. He came in and said that they didn't allow shooting in the town but he didn't think there were enough men in the town to stop them. One of these fairies would stand at one end of the hall and hold a whiskey glass over her head, and one of the cowboys would shoot it out of her hand, and he did it several times. One of these girls was so scared that she left town and went out on the prairie, and when they found her they asked her why she ran away, and she said she had been shot once and a burned child is afraid of fire.

Next day Jimmie and another boy were going down the street, when they heard music. When they located the house it was coming from, they stopped in front of the door. It was a girl who was playing (but not one of the fairies) and one boy said to the other, "Let's go in," and the girl jumped up and Jimmie stuck his foot in the door so she couldn't shut it. While she was trying to shut the door, the boys convinced her that they would do no harm, so she let them in. They behaved themselves and thanked her for playing and got up and went out. It was time for us to go back to camp on the other side of the river. One of the boys was so drunk, he had to be taken home. On the way he tried to jump out of the skiff and they tried to hold him in. Finally they told him, "Jump out and see if we care"; and he said, "I'll fool you; I won't do it."

Our next trip was down the river to the mouth of the Grand River, then up the river. We had to go through Sitting Bull's camp on the Grand River, and they weren't going to let us go through, and they were going to stop us. Running Antelope was the Chief and he was going to hold us up. I knew him years before and he asked me what we were doing, and why all the men and horses. I told him we were rounding up cattle. He said he thought we should pay him for going through the reservation. He also said whenever the Indians went east the white men made them pay for everything, and they thought that we should do the same. I told him that I couldn't pay him anything as I was working the same as the rest of the boys. Then he wanted to know where the boss was. Bill at that time was foreman. I told him what Antelope wanted, and Bill said to tell him that we didn't own the outfit and that he was working the same as the rest. Major McLaughlin was agent at that time and we had a pass to go through the reservation. When I told the Indians, they wanted to see the pass as they knew McLaughlin's signature. Bill showed them the pass, and they said it would be all right. After we had gone a short way, Running Antelope came up and stopped us. He wanted something to eat, if we didn't have any money. Each wagon gave him some grub and he went off satisfied.

Sioux horsemen in front of a store in Timmer

Making Good Money And Losing It Too in the 1880s

Charlie Colgrove

Holy God! The grass was good.

Charlie Colgrove was born in Australia in 1861. His father, a native of Vermont, was a sailor who served on whalers. His mother was from Edinburgh, Scotland. The Colgroves emigrated to Australia where they farmed and "dug gold." When Charlie was eight years old, the family returned to the United States with $4,000 in gold and settled near Hamilton, Missouri, just east of Kansas City. In 1880 Charlie's father and older brother, Bill, went to Bismarck where they worked as carpenters, and the next year, Charlie followed. In 1882 Charlie and Bill headed for Dickinson because, in Charlie's words, "we had the ranch idea in our heads."

MY FATHER WAS PRETTY HANDY with his hands so he thought he would take a trip up the Missouri and make some money on carpenter work, so in 1880 he and my oldest brother, Bill, came up the Missouri on an old steamship to Bismarck, Dakota Territory. Father worked on steamships, fixing and the like, and Bill worked on the railroad bridge at Bismarck. Back then the railroad track just went to the river bank, and then you trucked across the ice in winter. Finally the railroad laid tracks across the ice of the Missouri and on into Sully Springs. That's right out here near Medora in the Badlands, and the government had supplies there. Sully was just a shack, and the railroad put up a section house there. Towns sprung up like mushrooms pretty near ahead of the construction crews, and this looked like a pretty busy place. Lots of fellers came to work on the railroad. They thought it was something fine when the track went into Sully and a big day when the train pulled through. The railroad ran just two trains a day, one this way, one that.

My brother, Bill, had written about the big doings out here, so in 1881 I came out to Bismarck. Then an immigrant train came through along in July 1882, and Bill and I took it for Dickinson because there was so dang many buffalo bones to gather here, and we had the ranch idea in our heads. The immigrant trains had two coaches and seven or eight box cars hauling freight. It was so hot and smelly in that train. Lord God! You just couldn't stand that smell, so Bill and I got out at a stop and got on top of a box car to ride. Bill heard some coyotes down here near Gladstone, and he was scared. He thought the Indians were going to hold us up.

In the early days the railroad had a 40-mile grant through here on each side of the track. Well, Holy God! The railroad had a contract with the government to put a railroad clean through here and then it took ten years to get the land on the market — for 50 cents an acre. That was a pretty fair price, and it went like hot cakes, I'll tell you.

Well, now, Dickinson wasn't much in them early days — just a railroad section house, a few shacks, and the old Villard Hotel. I got my first schooner of real beer there — only cost a nickel, too, and it was a good big glass. Then, all along the streets, you saw stacks of buffalo hides, piled up for shipping; fellers riding Indian ponies; and families coming in wagons. In 1883 a caravan of thirteen came in one day to Dickinson. This was a damn good country for buffalo, and hides brought a fat price, I believe $2.00 per. Them buffalo bones laid all over this here country. Holy God! There was tons of them. I just picked big bones and left the little ones for the Russian kids in the country. I got $10.00 a load.

I've roamed all over these hills and prairies and been out in all kinds of weather. Always slept outdoors under a tarp, rain or shine. One time in November of 1883 I got caught in a snowstorm and, in the morning, had two feet of snow over me. Had to work like the devil to get out and get the old team going on their way. Well, that time you couldn't make any headway because you couldn't see the horses' heads ahead of you. A feller didn't have to worry about getting caught in a fence them days, so you could let the horses find their way. Wasn't no such thing as a fence. Along in '83 there was another storm and about the worst storm that was ever known. Lasted about an hour, but it sure raised the devil while it lasted. It was a wind and hail storm and blew down about all claim shacks that had sprung up around the country. Minnesota, Iowa, and Wisconsin had real tornadoes when we had the wind storm here, so we were pretty lucky.

Along in May 1883, 3,000 hides were brought in for shipping, and I've heard tell that a total of 250,000 buffalo hides were shipped in 1883. Also in '83 a herd of about 600 antelope was seen near town here.

Now 1886 was the year the snow blew. There's been many a bad spring since then, but none like old '86.

In '82 brother Bill and I started a ranch, the old Lime Kiln Ranch, just off in those big hills northeast of Lefor, about six or seven miles east of Black Butte. Then we started another ranch on Thirty-Mile Creek. That one was five or six miles from our old Lime Kiln Ranch. Holy God! The grass was good; we'd get 1,000 tons of hay a year and had plenty of grazing for 400 head of cattle on each ranch. With all the family filing on claims, we had the two sections we bought and school sections — 1,500 acres. At the Lime Kiln Ranch, we got closed out on ranching in 1906 because the damn farmers came in and run us out. That damn Iowa outfit was about the worst. There was lots of them, and they grabbed all the good land. Land around there sold for $2.00 an acre, but after they came it run up to $15.00 an acre. We had plenty water and good grazing. I got some fellers to file on homesteads and then traded them out of it for a couple of old horses, a saddle, or something. By God! A feller worked everything to get what he wanted.

The first cattle we bought were 225 head Black Angus. By God! They were pretty cattle — got them for $35.00 a head — calves thrown in. I put a damn stiff price on them and shipped to the St. Paul market. We made money on 'em. We never kept any old stuff — nothing over four years old. Got to running a herd of 1,000 head, between the two ranches.

We worked plenty hard in them days. Spent long hours on the range, and living conditions weren't any too good. Out on Lime Kiln Ranch we had a great big spring and a stone shack ten by twelve made of stones from our place. While we dug our basement, we dug up the skeleton of a white man who had a tin plate stuck in the back of his head. He'd been put there by Indians. That country used to be a great place for Sioux Indians. Their graves were all around the hills, and we found many a trinket of theirs around. About in 1886 I hauled lime from the old ranch to Dickinson to use in building the courthouse. I made a good lot of money in '86. I'd haul lime to Dickinson and pick bones going back. The Craven Indians [Gros Ventres] used to go through here too. Sometimes the Crow Indians came, but not so many. They bought meat and traded things for their beaded belts and other things. One day they drove in with a good mare and colt. I had a pretty good looking team myself, but they were damned balky. I never told them that, but they couldn't wait to get the trade across. They had an awful time to get started. One old horse kicked and raised the devil, but they got as far as Sully Springs, when one of the horses dropped dead. They got back here and waited till I got in from bone picking to kill me. We had a big fight, but I never got a scratch. The Indian had a one-sided nose and few other bumps.

I sold my interest in Lime Kiln Ranch to Bill and my father. Kept my interest in the Thirty-Mile Ranch and in 1887 started a 1,000-head sheep ranch two and one-half miles south of the Stark County line, or a little southeast of Dickinson.

In those early days there was plenty of freight outfits here, going between Dickinson, Belfield, and the Black Hills. George Mussey of New England was one of the freighters. I freighted for a while under Captain Fountain. There were three regiments camped here at Dickinson. Yes, sir! Captain Fountain had charge of them, and he sure knew his stuff. He had three Indians he brought with him from Montana, and he always sent an Indian ahead of us freighters to scout. He thought Indians would stop us, and he knew an Indian wouldn't shoot an Indian. I got ten dollars a day when I freighted one hundred miles. That was damn tiresome work, and then a feller always had to sleep out under the big sky, listen to coyotes howl, and be on the lookout for rattlers. Them big freight outfits had 30 to 40 wagons. There was one outfit had 30 head of oxen, and the boss rode horseback. They were the best trained oxen you about ever saw. One time when I was freighting I got caught in a storm in the Hills and didn't get out for ten days. There were some other fellers, but we all came damn near freezing and starving to death as well as the horses and mules in the outfit as the food and hay played out.

There were two doctors out in this country in early days, Dr. McDonald and Dr. Stickney. Often we'd meet them on the way to Dickinson. In them days they rode horseback.

Along in '85 I went up around Belfield some. That town had one store then and a few shacks. The fellers called the store "Penny-Anty Store." The feller that ran it was a stingy devil. I helped bury the first two fellers that died in Belfield — one feller's name was Tommy Rice, and I can't remember the other one. George Old had a lot about where the Belfield Depot stands now, and I dug the first well in Belfield. Got just black water. Guess it was all coal there. Then Bill Tuttle out north of Belfield wanted me to dig a well on his place. I did it for him, and 25 feet down ran into a layer of buffalo bones.

We had great times when all the cowpunchers got together and celebrated. We'd set around, swap yarns, drink a little, and compare six-shooters. I sure had a good one and was a pretty good shot. A feller was pretty proud of a buffalo gun and six-shooter in them days.

Just west of Belfield Ole Murry had a claim in the Badlands. Ole was from Minnesota, and his wife wouldn't come out here in this wild country. One summer she came out for a visit, and the cowhands decided to celebrate. About ten of us got together and rode out horseback. We shot off the house shingles and rode around the house and yelled. We thought they'd take it for a joke, but Ole's wife left the next day. She had enough of this wild west. We felt pretty bad about that.

One night while I was sleeping out on the prairie south of Belfield a cub bear came up and licked my ear. Guess he thought it was a sugar-cured ham. I sure got up in a hurry. My horse was throwing its head around and acting up. Then two big bears showed up. They were pretty tame though, but I was glad when they wandered off.

Well, the Gladstone country was growing faster than Dickinson, but some of us fellers pulled for Dickinson and got a county seat here.

Lee of Gladstone, H.L. Dickinson, and a feller named Underhill were the first county commissioners. Bill Cuskelly was the first sheriff, and I was on the first jury. It was along in October 1887. The first cases we had were for horse stealing in the Badlands, cattle rustling, and cases against a couple of women for houses of ill-fame.

The slough grass in this country made the best hay you about ever saw, and a feller could put up a ton of hay in no time. Holy God! I've raked many a ton with a hand rake. That was before we had mowers — the first one I bought cost $95.00. I had it for nine years, and I took plenty good care of it, and wouldn't cut a buffalo bone or nothing with it. Well, I had 50 tons of hay one time that got caught in prairie fires. Never did find out how the damn fire started. Them days you kinda expected things to happen. A feller kinda thought who it was, but there wasn't much fuss. A feller always thought the day would come when he could pay back.

Lord, God! We made good money in them early days. We had some big losses too, but nothing like some of the outfits. We had some good hills that gave pretty good protection to cattle, and we made a few shelter sheds around. The railroad brought in a bunch of old ties and snow fences. Sometimes if a feller needed a board, he'd get one off a snow fence. We hauled a bunch of old ties, and once in a while a feller accidentally got a new one. Well, when you put ties with mud and straw with a sod roof, it didn't take nothing to build sheds. But most of the stuff was turned out on the range and let run. Our stuff was always in pretty good shape till them damn farmers got coming in and made hay short. Now, them Texas fellers sure tried to get all this country, but they sure brought in some good stuff. Some them fellers would drive a herd of cattle from Texas and start in the spring and never get here till fall. When they did get here, them cattle was poor as Job's turkey. They'd get in pretty fair shape over the winter, but lots of them died. I don't know what their notion was, but they'd bring in steers six-seven years old, and they never would get any meat on 'em. Four years old is plenty old to keep a steer because you always get a price then.

The Hash-Knife out from Texas was in here about half way between Dickinson and the Black Hills. Their cattle, between three and four thousand head, had a hash-knife brand on their shoulders. In '86, the year the snow blew — I'll never forget it, old '86 — the Hash-Knife outfit lost 500 head. There was just one damn blizzard after another. I lost plenty that year, too, but nothing like some fellers. One day in '86 a feller named Taminlin, who had a claim down south of here about ten miles, brought a load of hay to Dickinson on a wagon hitched to two old nags. That same day the Hash-Knife outfit was in here drinking and shooting up the town, and old Taminlin got right on a street corner when the Hash-Knifers took a few pops at him. Taminlin seemed to go right down in the hay, and one horse was killed. After the shooting let up, old Taminlin crawled out and said, "Well, why didn't they get old Ted, too?" He got a good horse from the Hash-Knife outfit for the one they killed. That outfit would raise hell and tear things galley-west, then pay back for any damage they had done to anyone. They were pretty good that way.

About the same time a couple of German fellers, August and George Beisigle, came to me and asked me to put in a ranch for them 25 miles northwest of Dickinson. George was a fine feller, but August was a stingy devil. They used to say he'd go shipping and put two crackers in his pocket and come back with one. He was that stingy. Well, Holy God! I went out the Beisigle land with a Hungarian feller. It was a plenty good grazing country. We dug a well 25 feet deep, cut cottonwoods, and made a log house besides fixing places for cattle to drink. We were there three weeks and worked like the devil to get everything done. We had pretty fair ponies and quite a bit of grub, but we ran out of salt. A feller wouldn't believe it, but, By God! I wanted salt worse than anything in the world just then. Next we ran out of flour, so we took the coffee grinder and ground oats. If you ever swallowed fish hooks, you know about what it tasted like. We killed a deer there too, but without salt it wasn't fit to eat.

The 25th day of November '86 we started back to Dickinson, plodded through two feet of snow, and the dang ponies played out when we got to Indian Springs. We rolled up in tarps, and the next day you could hardly find us. November 26 we managed to reach Dickinson, and I decided I'd had enough helping other fellers. Holy God! There was always somebody after you to do something.

A feller that used to be in and out of here in early days was Calamity Joe. Did you ever hear of Calamity? Well, Calamity's real name was Joe Meyers, and he was from down around Hebron. He was a drinker and was usually around the saloon here. Calamity stole thirteen head of Indian ponies and was shot by the Deputy Sheriff. Everybody thought Calamity would die, but he managed to pull through and went out west. In a couple of years he was back with 25 head of horses. Nobody ever knew for sure where he got 'em, but we always figured he got 'em on Buffalo Range down on Grand River in the Black Hills. He sure got some good stuff.

Them early days a feller could go to the First National Bank here in Dickinson and get all the money he needed to buy sheep and cattle. A Hilliard was the banker, and he sure trusted a feller. Damn it! They sure wouldn't do it now days. The banking game is all different, but they ain't making money either like they did in them days.

Now my brother, Bill, and I were about the only fellers doing ranching in '83 south of here. Father liked the layout, too; so he quit working and went in on the Lime Kiln Ranch.

Some of the nearly 700,000 sheep in North Dakota in 1900

Ranchers in this country hated sheep, but I did pretty well in the sheep game. On the sheep ranch I ran 1,000 sheep, then I got it up to 2,000 head, and finally up to 3,000. I put a lot out on shares. I remember the bunch I put out on shares in '88 to a feller south of Sentinel Butte. I got $400.00 worth of sheep shot up because the fellers out there didn't want them. Holy God! I was mad about that. I made good money and took good care of the sheep. Never kept one over five years old. A feller who doesn't know nothing about sheep can't do with 'em.

I followed the ranching game till the farmers got too damn thick. I've always said the government should have never opened up the Badlands for settlement, but should have left it for cattlemen.

The year the snow blew, 1886, I married Kate Gubson — she's German. I picked buffalo bones all day before we was married and got $10.00 for the load. Paid the justice $5.00 and bought flour with the other $5.00. Well, we never took no wedding trip or nothing — just went out to the shack at the ranch on Lime Creek. I left Kate and started picking bones the next day. I'd been a damn good spender till Kate got a hold of me. I remember hearing about a wedding down at Gladstone that old Grover Jopp performed. He was Justice of Peace at Gladstone. Jopp had a couple who wanted to get married, and he asked 'em if they had the $5.00 fee. They said, "Yes," so Jopp hunted for his book. When he did find it, he couldn't find the place. "Damn it," he said. "Oh, give me the $5.00. You're married. That's good enough." Kate and I raised a fair-sized family and a durn good one.

This God-dang country suits me. Now, when I was a young feller, I went down into Texas to see about buying some cattle. Now, I was down in Wyoming, too; and no Wyoming for me. North Dakota had plenty storms, but no Dakota storm ever fazed me. The time I was down in Wyoming, down in the Pine Hills, a God-dang sand storm come up and beat anything North Dakota ever had. So I said right there, I'm going back to North Dakota, pick out some good stuff that's brought there, and stay.

I knew Bill Follis, who rode this whole dang country. He was the foreman for a big outfit, the 777. One of their last big drives was made along in 1898 to Eland Stock Yards just west of Dickinson three miles. They shipped something like six or seven thousand.

Bill was on a roundup once going through the reservation, and he saw Sitting Bull and his boy. They just had a shack, and Sitting Bull couldn't read, but the boy could. Bill said that he was going down the main trail and had six good ponies with him when he looked up and saw Indians all over a hill nearby. He figured they wanted his ponies and wasn't much surprised when Sitting Bull and his boy appeared and stopped him. They wanted his permit to go on the reservation, so Bill gave one to him, and the boy said he should take other trail or a cutoff. Bill told them that he got that far on the trail he was on, and it was good enough for him. Bill says those dang Indians disappeared in a gulch, and he went on down the trail. It's a good thing Bill kept going or he would never had had those six ponies.

I never had much trouble with Indians, but once when I was going down to the Black Hills freighting, I bought a couple cow hides from a feller to make blankets out of. They were as pretty a hide as you'll ever see. Well, anyway, the next morning I thought I heard a noise so jumped up quick, and there was a damn squaw running around the wagon with one of my hides. First I thought I'd chase her and get the hide back, but then I figured I'd get popped off by some Indians hiding in the hills so I let her go. I sure hated to let them have that hide. Yes, sir! That's once I took a skinning.

I knowed all the fellers that trailed in here with cattle. Oh, God, them days it was easy to know everybody. Course there wasn't so many to know. A fellow just stopped and started talking and was glad to see a newcomer. Them days everybody liked to tell where he was from and how he left things where he come from. According to most of them, they left quite a bit to come here.

All the fellers used to have roundups together, and then at the end of the roundup they'd throw everything together and get the stuff that wasn't branded together. All the cowboys would have a chance at roping and could claim the stuff they got a hold of. The cowboys used to like that part of the roundups. Some of them were pretty fair with the rope and could do pretty good.

Ranching Near New Rockford in Lonesome Country

The Fay Family

I went outside the shanty and shouted "Hello" just to hear the echo and to break the endless silence.

The Fay family's odyssey represented a familiar four-generation pattern: Ireland to New Hampshire to Illinois to Dakota. J.C. Fay was born in 1860 at Rockford, Illinois, where he graduated from high school. After taking a course of study at a Chicago business school, he worked as a bookkeeper at his father's soap and fertilizer factory in Mendota, Illinois. In 1880 he married twenty-year-old Caroline Elizabeth whose family had moved from New York to Michigan to Illinois. Two years later J.C. and his father caught "cattle fever" and headed for Dakota to find suitable land for a ranch; they located near New Rockford in Cherry Lake Township. They stayed on the ranch until 1892 when Fay was elected sheriff of Eddy County. He later ran a grocery store and grain-buying business in New Rockford. Although the Fays avoided many frontier hardships because of the family's monied position, they could not, as Caroline Elizabeth Fay remembers, avoid the loneliness or the ravages of weather.

THE MEN FOLKS CAME FIRST with several emigrant cars. They covered their houses with sheet iron which they brought with them from Mendota (the pieces were riveted together). This was a good protection from the storms in the summer, but I would rather be blown up the hill in a cyclone than to live in a house covered with sheet iron again. It drew the heat in the summer and the frost in the winter. The walls used to be dripping wet most of the time in cold weather. When the men came through Chicago, J.C. Fay's father bought fur coats, robes, leggings, and gauntlets so everyone in the Fay family had a fur coat to wear. They brought food supplies enough to last a couple of years including barrels of sugar, salt, lard, molasses, cases of apricots, peaches and evaporated apples, prunes in the hundred pound sacks, and 2,500 pounds of meat (salted, smoked, summer sausage, blood sausage, pickled meats, etc.).

They also brought 40 head of cattle, 20 head of horses, hogs, poultry, feed, machinery, and household furniture. The men were three days covering the 69 mile trip from Jamestown to the ranch with the stock and supplies.

We women arrived a little later. Mr. Fay met us in Jamestown and we came across the country in a covered wagon. We passed only one settler's house between Jamestown and Larabee. We stopped at Cummings' for coffee and then went on to Larabee where we stayed overnight at Captain Warren's home and then went the remaining ten miles to the Fay ranch. This trip took three days, and we never met a soul on the road.

Antelope came up to our door to feed. They grew tame with the cattle. I have often seen the ground snow white with wild geese. I learned from an old trapper that young crane stuffed and roasted was much better than goose. We often had this dish.

I hitched old Lucy to the wagon and took the two little boys, Ben and Charles, down in the ravine to gather buffalo bones. It got dark almost before we knew it, and I didn't know the way home. I tried to be brave; I didn't want to let the children know I was afraid. Little Ben said, "Let's just give old Lucy the line like the men do and she'll take us home." Lucy did.

Upon arriving home from gathering buffalo bones, I tried to hurry the fire with a little kerosene. There wasn't much left in the can but that can blew into a thousand pieces. My clothes caught on fire and fire singed my hair. I grabbed a blanket, threw it around me, and rolled on the floor until the flames were put out.

Many times when I first came to Dakota I went outside the shanty and shouted "Hello" for recreation just to hear the echo and to break that endless silence.

*Bill Conneley horse and cattle ranch near
Dunn Center, Dakota, 1887*

Our place seemed to be the stopping place for travelers. It seemed I was cooking all the time. I used to bake twenty loaves of bread every second day. We carried water from a barrel sunk in a low place where the water was near the surface. We boiled and strained it before we used it. I was here four years without seeing the railroad. Then in 1887 I rode to New Rockford on a load of potatoes to have a tooth drawn by Dysinger from Minnewaukan; to my sorrow he pulled the wrong tooth.

The Scandinavians had a colony by themselves in the hills about five miles from our place. One day I saw a woman coming over the snow, moving her hands rapidly. When she came nearer, I could see that she was knitting as she walked. She had come for medicine and brought a large piece of beef in payment. We could not understand each other, but I made coffee and through much pantomime I learned that someone had a fever and she wanted medicine. I gave her belladonna and acouite which with laudanum and sweet spirits of nitre were the old standbys of the early settlers.

I think the sunsets and the Northern Lights are beautiful here in Dakota. Flowers grew in great abundance. The lady slippers, jack in the pulpit, and blue bells were everywhere. Ben and Charlie often filled a wash tub with tiger lilies as a gift.

We used to sit and scrape buffalo bones with a piece of sharp glass for hours just to pass the time. Then we polished them with a soft cloth or chamois until they would just shine. We used them for ornaments and sometimes for legs on footstools.

Many Indians with their squeaking carts drawn by little Indian ponies passed by our door on the Old Fort Totten Trail.

I had heard many stories about the Indians. The first time they passed our house, the wheels of their carts were stained crimson to the hubs from the crushed wild strawberries along the trail. I was almost paralyzed with fear. I thought it was blood.

Soldiers were still stationed at Fort Totten in 1883, but the Indians were considered peaceable. I remember one of the squaws had a horrible scar on her face. It was said she had been a traitor and that this was the evidence of her punishment. An old Indian by the name of Blue Shield always had a ready smile and cordial greeting for everyone.

I shall never forget the first powwow I witnessed. The carts were drawn into a circle, and the fire in the center cast weird shadows as the dancers leaped and swayed about until they fell exhausted. They were painted in glaring colors and decked out with feathers. Our friend in the East offered to send firearms for our protection, for the papers were full of hair-raising tales of the savages in the West. However, they never harmed us.

The worst storm I ever saw came on March 8, 1892. For several days we had been having balmy spring weather, and the snowbanks which had been piled mountain high were rapidly diminishing. During the day we had a warm drizzling rain and a southeast wind. About half past six that evening there was a dead stop to the breeze, but within an hour a gale was sweeping down from the northwest with a heavy downfall of snow. It continued all night and all the next day.

Ole Larson who lived out near Brantford had gone to town and had started back before the storm struck but failed to reach home. He was found after the storm. He had perished from exhaustion and suffocation.

I was almost frantic; Mr. Fay had left for town early that morning with a load of grain. He knew it wasn't safe to start for home so waited until the storm let up the morning of the second day. It was getting toward evening of the second day; I made the children promise they wouldn't go near the fire, and I started out walking to hunt for him. I was only two or three miles from home when I found one of the blankets he had lost. Then I was just sure I would find Charlie's dead body.

I walked seven miles, then I looked through the field-glass I had taken with me. In the distance I could see a team coming and sure enough it was Charlie and the mules.

We had over 80 head of fine beef and milk cows. During the storm they broke out of the corral and wandered away. When we found them, all but two or three had been suffocated by the blinding snow. Thousands of cattle perished in the state. Old pets we brought with us from Michigan lay dead. I tell you it was heart breaking.

My first recreation after coming to Dakota was a ball game and a picnic in People's Grove on the Sheyenne River in June 1885. On our way over, a cloud burst frightened the team into running away.

Bill Maiv, his wife, and children were along with us. When the horses started running, Charlie told us to jump. In doing so my wrist was broken. One of the players, Wilfred Maiv, made a sling of his stocking and I witnessed the game. That evening we drove to New Rockford and Dr. McLachlin and a doctor who was visiting there set the break.

We used to take 200 and 300 pounds of butter a week to Carrington and sell it to Strong-Chase for 20 to 25 cents per pound. Finally they didn't want to give us but 15 cents per pound for our butter and wanted us to take that in trade, so we quit making butter and let the calves run with the cows instead of milking them.

Land Locator, Cowboy, Sheepherder

Rueben Humes

We worked from sunup to sundown.

Rueben Humes' mother died in 1883 when he was only three years old. His father gave up his job as a carpenter in Peoria, Illinois, and homesteaded near Redfield, Dakota Territory. In 1892 his father disappeared, and Rueben stayed with his grandparents and herded sheep for $20.00 a month. In 1897 at age seventeen Rueben began "bumming" his way through the South, but finding wages low, he returned to Dakota and located in Dickinson where a young energetic man had no difficulty finding jobs.

IN 1907 MANY SETTLERS WERE COMING into Dickinson, looking for homesteads. I made considerable money helping the settlers get located. I acted as guide and furnished a team and a two-seated buggy. I received seven dollars for each day I was out. The settlers paid all expenses on the trip such as hay and feed for the horses. On some of these trips I would be out in the country six or seven days before the settler would find a homestead that suited him. Some trips took us almost to the South Dakota line. At night we would stay at a ranch or some deserted shack or sleep out in the open. Food on these trips consisted of bacon, bologna, canned tomatoes, bread, and coffee.

The ranchers did not like to see the settlers come in, especially foreigners. If I went near a ranch with a load of foreigners, they usually bawled me out and told me to take them away, the farther the better. The worst experience I had was with three Finlanders. They hired me to take them out late in the fall. We left Dickinson about five o'clock in the morning and traveled south. They were very surly, and as they could not talk any English, I had a hard time to understand them. After we were about five miles out of Dickinson one of the men pulled out a bottle of whiskey. From that time on they were drunk all the time. As soon as one bottle was empty they pulled out another. They offered me a drink from time to time, but I would not drink. They started arguing with each other, and the next minute the two men in the back seat started to fight. I was afraid they would break the buggy seat, so I stopped and pulled them out on the ground. After fighting about half an hour, they both had enough. They quit and got back in the buggy. After a few more drinks the fighting started again. This time all three of them were engaged. I was so disgusted I tried to go back to Dickinson, but they did not want to go. I then decided to try and sober them up. We were near a creek that ran into the Heart River, and in place of taking the regular crossing where the river could be forded easily, I drove two miles east. The stream was four or five feet deep at this place. I drove the horses into the water. As the water came up over the buggy, the men started to yell. We all got wet. The bank on the other side of the river was steep and bumpy. The buggy hit a bump just as it came out of the river. One of the men was bumped out backwards and hit the mud with his head. This sort of sobered them up. We built a fire and dried our clothes. I could tell they were angry at me, but I did not care. I then drove on a few more miles, then circled around and went back to Dickinson. They did not want to go, but I had enough of them. I drove up to the livery stable. They got out of the buggy and started to walk off. I yelled and motioned at them to come back, as I had not been paid. They kept right on walking. I had just started after them when Abe Morse and five of his men from the Stone Ranch rode up. They wanted to know what the trouble was as they had heard me yelling. I told them I had not been paid. They took after the Finlanders on horseback. As they rode, they let out a few warhoops. The Finlanders heard them and stopped. They knew the men were coming after them, and they were badly frightened. The men rode around in front of them and motioned for them to go back to the barn. They did not lose any time coming back to me and paid up in full. That was the last I ever saw of them.

In the hills around Dickinson in 1900 there were coyotes, gray and buffalo wolves, and bobcats. There were not so many buffalo wolves, but they were the largest and the most dangerous. These animals caused considerable damage to the stock and sheep men by killing cattle, sheep, and horses. Coyotes killed sheep just to be killing, while the gray and buffalo wolves usually just killed one or two sheep at a time. The wolves ate what they killed, while the coyotes would leave ten or fifteen slaughtered sheep.

Bobcats usually attacked lambs that wandered away from the flock. A cat would jump on a lamb and knock it to the ground. It then bit a hole through the lamb's side and sucked the blood from the heart and lungs. Bobcats very seldom ate any of the flesh.

Gray and buffalo wolves would also attack horses, colts, cattle, and calves. The wolves would hamstring these animals to make them helpless, then kill them by biting through the jugular vein in the throat. They killed all these animals, but they liked colt meat the best. Many of the horses around Dickinson showed marks where wolves had tried to hamstring them. Wolves sometimes became so bold that they would go in a barn at night and try to hamstring a horse.

In order to help protect the ranchers, the state paid a bounty of $20.00 for each wolf killed. The ranchers' association paid an additional $10.00.

The first buffalo wolf I ever saw almost scared me to death. I was working at the Stone Ranch at the time and was out in a camp with some other men. I had the afternoon off, so I decided to go out and try to get a chicken or two for supper. We had a sixteen gauge shot gun in camp. The firing pin did not work right on the gun, and sometimes it would miss firing three or four times. I started out on foot and walked about two miles to the Heart River without seeing any chickens. Just as I arrived in a horseshoe bend in the river, a covey of chickens flew up. I shot and one of the birds fell on the other side of the river. To get the chicken I had to walk about a quarter of a mile down the river to a cattle ford in order to get across as the banks were so steep. Just as I reached the top bank near the crossing, I saw something on the other side of the river. It looked like a big black sheep. It was gray and had a huge mane of hair. I was so surprised I just stopped and looked. About that time the animal started for the ford, and I saw that it was the largest wolf I had ever seen. I thought the wolf had seen me and was coming for me. I was badly scared as I had no confidence in the gun at all, but I knew I could use it as a club if I was compelled. I backed up a few feet and held the gun ready to shoot. The wolf came right on up the path toward me. The head of the wolf was close to the ground and as it came near me I could see its eyes. Its tongue curled out around the side of his mouth and it was very ugly. Just as the wolf reached the top of the bank I pulled the trigger, but the gun misfired. I don't know if the wolf had seen me until then or not. The wolf turned to the left and rode the wind. Back in camp the men told me it was a buffalo wolf.

At this time there were thousands of grouse in the hills. Antelope were plentiful. They were protected by law, but this did not do much good as the homesteaders, ranchers, and hunters shot them for food.

There were lots of rattlesnakes, but we got so used to them that we did not pay much attention to them. Many nights when I slept out in the open, I could hear snakes rattling all around, but I figured one place was as good as another, so I did not move my bed. The only precaution we took was to shake our boots in the morning.

In the fall of the year I shot many grouse with a .22 rifle. I would go out early in the morning along the Heart River or some creek. I would find a large cottonwood tree that was located near a patch of bull-berries. I would build a blind about 30 or 35 yards from the cottonwood tree. To make a blind I would make a depression in the ground and cover it with branches and grass. I crawled into the blind and waited for the grouse to come. Sometimes hundreds of them would light in the cottonwood tree. I shot the grouse that were on the lower branches and worked up. I shot the grouse in the head, and as long as they tumbled to the ground, the other grouse would not fly away, but if I just wounded one and it flew away, the others would usually follow. In half an hour or so more chickens would light in the tree. Some mornings I would kill as high as 50 chickens. I kept a few and sold the others for 15 cents each in Dickinson. They were packed and shipped east.

I hired out to the Stone Ranch in 1900. I had worked on farms at various times, but ranching was altogether different. I was given a bunk in the bunkhouse and told to make myself at home. About a dozen cowboys were in the bunkhouse. They were all happy and good natured. It did not take them long to start calling me Rube. They figured I was a green hand, and they kidded me plenty, but it was all in fun, so I did not get mad. Early the next morning we were up and making preparations for the fall roundup.

The horse wrangler had driven about 50 head of horses into the corral. The foreman, Abe Morse, pointed out five horses that I was to use. I was given a saddle, bridle, and a rope. The foreman told me to catch and saddle one, and he walked away. As the horses were milling around, I could not tell what horses were supposed to be mine. I walked over and managed to catch a horse with a rope. The horse dashed away. I tried to hold it, but the rope pulled through my hands, burning them plenty. By this time the other men had their horses all saddled and were watching me. One of the men called out, "Rube, that's the worse bronc in the bunch. He would throw you over the corral." The men then helped me get the rope off the horse and then caught and saddled a horse for me. The foreman then came up and gave us orders. He told each man to ride a certain group of hills or a certain creek. As I was green he sent me with a man named Edwards. He told us where the cook car could be located. The cattle were grazing within a radius of 20 miles from the ranch. Edwards and I rode along at a slow trot, and once in a while we let the horses walk. As we rode along, Edwards pointed out landmarks to me. We passed bunches of cattle. They were wild. Edwards told me that if ever I was caught on foot, the cattle would chase me if I tried to run away but would not harm me if I did not run. This advice came in handy later on.

We started our drive about 20 miles from the ranch. Edwards took one side of the creek, and I took the other side. That day we ate a cold lunch consisting of roast beef and some dough biscuits. We carried water in canteens. As we rode the creek, we each found about 50 cattle.

Toward evening we came to the camp. Altogether we had gathered about 750 head. We drove ours into the herd and went in to eat supper. I could hardly walk when I got off the horse. We ate a supper consisting of fried beef, canned tomatoes, canned peaches, coffee, and sourdough biscuits. After supper I was told I could go to bed and get some rest. I was given some blankets and slept on the ground. I was so tired I went to sleep at once. About one o'clock in the morning I was awakened by one of the boys and told to ride herd. The cattle were all down, and but two of us were on guard. I was sore and stiff and ached all over. I rode herd about two hours and then got about one hour's rest before breakfast. We had some dough pancakes, coffee, and beefsteak for breakfast. The foreman then sent most of us out again in different directions. We brought in about 500 more cattle. I was in misery throughout the day, and the saddle stirrups wore the skin from my legs. The next day we cut out the steers and branded calves. The boss let me work with the branding iron so I did not have to do any riding. Some of the cattle had brands of a different ranch. The other ranches sent one or two men to our camp so they could brand their calves.

The roundup lasted about five days. We drove the cows and steers to Dickinson, a distance of about 60 miles. We grazed them along slowly. It took us about a week to reach Dickinson. The cook wagon followed along behind us. At night we slept on the ground. By this time I was getting used to being in the saddle for 15 or 18 hours a day.

After we had loaded the cattle in freight cars in Dickinson, the men were paid off. They proceeded at once to get drunk in the blind pigs. They had a noisy good time. Some took part in poker games. We spent one day in Dickinson loafing. Morse then told the men to be ready to leave the next morning. By this time most of the men were broke. We made the return trip in three days.

Very little hay was put up on the ranch because the cattle were wintered along the creeks. Our main work during the winter was to keep the cattle near creeks and keep the water holes open. In the spring we rode the range and pulled cattle out of holes. My horse got away from me on one of these occasions. I had just pulled a cow out of a bog hole and had just untied the rope when my horse ran away. I was about nine miles from the ranch house. I felt foolish as I started for the ranch on foot. Now and then I passed three or four head of cattle. They raised their heads and looked as if they were coming toward me, but I took my time passing them. One or two steers took a few steps toward me. I was scared that they would take after me. I took my time walking and the steers stopped and started to graze. After walking about two miles, I came upon about 50 head of cattle on the side of a hill. As soon as they saw me, every one raised their heads. I did not like the looks of them and started edging my way around them. I noticed that seven or eight of them left the herd and started after me. I did not like the looks of this situation at all. As they gained on me, I saw that the first one was an old bull. He let out a bellow when he was about 50 yards from me and started pawing the dirt.

I then stopped walking but the bull kept right on coming, bellowing and pawing the dirt. I knew I might just as well wait and see what would happen as to keep on walking. The bull kept coming until he was within 20 or 30 yards from me. He kept his head close to the ground and kept on pawing and every once in a while would let out a bellow. I stood still and did not make a move. I stood that way about five or ten minutes. I kept my eyes on the bull all the time. He did not come any closer. Some of the other cattle that had followed me turned aside and started to graze. I took a few steps and, as the bull did not follow, I kept on. I was hoping the bull would not follow, but no such luck. After I had covered about 35 yards, the bull came after me again. I stopped and the bull stopped. I moved and the bull moved. This kept up for over a mile and took one or two hours. Just at this time I was saved when one of the men, Fred Ristine, rode up leading my horse. For a few minutes I was so shaky I could hardly talk. Fred said he had found my horse and figured I had been thrown and hurt and had been looking for me. We then rode back to the ranch where I got a nice razzing from the boys who thought it was a good joke.

Even though we put in long hours, I liked the work on the ranch. I saved most of my money.

In 1903 the Stone Ranch went out of the cattle business, and I became a sheepherder. I did not like sheep but I liked to work on the sheep ranch or the Stone Ranch, so I decided to stay. The Stone Ranch purchased 6,000 sheep. The sheep were divided into three bands of

2,000 head each. Two men took care of one band. We had a sheep-herder's wagon. It was the same length as an ordinary wagon but it was built six feet wide. The bunk was built crosswise in the end of the wagon. Under the bunk was a compartment for clothes. Running lengthwise in the wagon on both sides were benches with an aisle through the center. A small wood-burning sheet-iron stove was used for cooking and warmth. The round top of the wagon was covered with a layer of oil cloth, then a layer of blankets and then a layer of canvas. This made a nice warm house in any kind of weather. We had two horses to pull the wagon.

Food consisted of sourdough pancakes, sourdough biscuits, bacon, mutton or beef, canned tomatoes, corn, peaches, and dried fruit. A camp tender brought out food from the ranch every two weeks.

We worked from sunup to sundown. At sunup in the morning the sheep started to graze. Our main work during the day was to keep the sheep spread apart so they would not eat all the grass. We had one dog, a Scotch-Collie, to work with. He helped us in driving the sheep. If any sheep wandered away too far, he brought them back. About once a day the sheep went to the creek for water. When one started, all the rest started and followed. About sundown we started rounding up the sheep and bedded them down near the camp wagon.

In June we drove the sheep to the ranch where they were sheared. We had an old goat to lead the sheep on long drives. We covered about twelve miles a day on a drive.

I did not do any shearing. The ranch hired shearers. A good shearer would shear one hundred or more sheep in one day and average seven to ten dollars a day in wages.

After the sheep were sheared, we took to the hills again. We grazed the sheep as far into the winter as the weather permitted. When the weather got too disagreeable, we drove the sheep to a camp where we had sheep sheds. The sheds were built of poles and covered with hay. We grazed the sheep on good days and fed the sheep in the shed on the bad days. We had a little shack to live in here.

The next spring during lambing time the weather was bad. It was cold, and it rained for ten days. We were wet practically this entire time.

Most of the lambs died, and the hill on which we threw the dead lambs looked like it was covered with snow.

This life was easy but it was tiresome, lonesome, and monotonous.

My worst experience in a blizzard occurred in 1904. I was herding sheep on the Stone ranch at the time. We had a hard winter with lots of snow. I was hoping we would have a few nice days so we could take the sheep out of the hills. Along in February the weather turned warmer, and I thought we were soon to get a break.

I told Ed Mahon, my partner, we would turn the sheep out on the first warm day. Two days later I had gone down to the creek and started to pry loose sandstone rock with a crowbar. I was going to use these to line our well. About eleven o'clock in the morning, I noticed Ed had the sheep out. They were on the ridges about two miles away. It was quite warm and I thought it was all right. In about half an hour great big snow flakes started to fall. I made a dash for the house and told Ed that we had to get the sheep under cover. As we walked out to where the sheep were, a wind started blowing from the north. We found out that we could not drive the sheep against the storm as the snowflakes blinded the sheep, and they would not move. I then sent Ed to our other camp, which was about two miles away, for help. I stayed with the sheep and tried to drive them. I smashed into the flock and pushed a few ahead. Then I pushed more sheep into the gap. I could not make any progress. Ed brought two men with him, and even then we could not move the sheep. I sent the men back to the camp to bring out a load of hay. We scattered this along the ground back to the camp, but the sheep would not follow it back.

By this time the storm was getting worse. The other two men went back to camp, but Ed and I stayed with the sheep. The sheep drifted with the storm. Every time a sheep drifted away from the flock, we grabbed it and carried it back again.

As the night wore on, the snow flakes became smaller and the wind colder. Our clothing and faces were covered with snow which turned into ice in the cold wind. The sheep were covered with snow about three inches thick. The snow melted and froze on their bodies until they were covered with ice.

By three o'clock in the morning we had followed the sheep seven miles. We were nearly exhausted and knew that we had to find a house soon. The wind had stopped, but it was terribly cold. We knew there were a few settlers living in the hills so we set out to find a house. By this time we were suffering from the intense cold. After wandering about three miles, we saw a light. Ed was in worse shape than I. He was just able to stagger along. On reaching the house I kicked on the door with my feet. Shortly a young man came to the door. He took one look at us, and then he reached out and pulled us in. He had us lie down on the floor and then pulled off our clothes. Up to this time I had not noticed much pain, but as the frozen spots on our faces and bodies thawed out, the pain was nearly unbearable.

Ed was in such bad shape that he could not stand up in the morning. Our flesh turned purple. The man in whose house we had stopped bundled us up in blankets and took us in a bobsled to our camp, as Ed was in bad shape, he was taken to a hospital in Dickinson. I did not do anything for a week myself. Out of our band of 1,800 sheep, at least half of them died out in the hills. Half of the rest died after they were brought back to the sheep sheds. The sheep were still covered with ice when they were driven into the sheds. In the sheds the ice slowly melted on the sheep. The cold water was more than the sheep could stand and about half of them died.

Ed came back from the hospital in 20 days. He did not look like the same person at all. His face was sunk in and full of holes.

On my face and body were about twenty spots covered with proud flesh where I had been frozen. These places would not heal so I was taken to Dickinson and put in the hospital. This was the end of sheep herding for me.

Ranching on the Souris River in McHenry County

John Inkster

I remember the first time I ever danced, and joined a lodge more because of the girls than because I wanted to be in the Good Templar Lodge.

Born in the Dakota town named by his father in 1879, John Inkster moved with his family to the Mouse River Loop about seven miles from Towner when he was three. He attended country schools and went for three or four years to live with his uncle in Winnipeg to go to school. He taught at the first school in Denbigh in 1897. That same year, his mother died while his father was in Alaska. John was recovering from spinal meningitis. He worked on the ranch and went to Archibald's Business College in Minneapolis in 1898-99.

FROM EARLY CHILDHOOD, I learned the way of ranches, and I was able to do any of the things that had to be done — build fences, break horses, rope, brand, make hay, and feed cattle in the winter time. I learned to have a good time on the ranch, too. I fished for suckers, pickerel, and pike — I got them when they came for air in the McIntyre Spring, about a mile from our home ranch. In the early days, fish were so thick in the Mouse River that we could shovel them out with pitchforks. I remember that when I was twelve or thirteen I speared a pickerel that weighed 35½ pounds. It was so strong that it nearly ran off with me. I saw it in open space, speared it, and it began to swim off. I jumped into the water after the fish, and after a short fight, I got it. That fish went on display at the Pendroy Meat Shop in Towner.

Log cabin built by George T. Inkster in 1878 where the family lived before moving to Towner County in 1882

from the Fred Hultstrand History in Pictures Collection, NDIRS-NDSU, Fargo

After I got back from business college, I still worked the ranch, and I even had a few cattle of my own. Then I went to Sherwood, a new frontier back then, because the railroad had just been built from Granville. I stayed there for three or four years.

My father took my mother, who was French and Indian, and me to the ranch about a mile from Hackett's Crossing. My father was the first white man in the Mouse River Loop. Our family brought about three wagons loaded with the things we would need, such as tools, household goods, and furniture.

The land around Towner was not surveyed until 1882, and my father, George Inkster, took what land he wanted. He built a log house with two rooms for us; it had a log floor and mud roof. The logs came from oak he got along the river. About three years later, he built an upstairs and shingled the roof. Until he could finish that first house from logs he hewed himself, we lived in tents.

We had to go to Devils Lake for supplies, because that was the end of the railroad then. We usually only made two trips a year because of the expense and distance — it was 75 miles to the lake. When we made the trip, we took two teams and brought back flour, sugar, salt, coffee, and dried fruit. I was grown up before I knew there was any kind of fruit besides prunes and dried apples. We raised potatoes, carrots, cabbage, rutabagas, and stored them in our root cellar. My mother made all the clothing, even our red-flannel underwear.

We got our first water from a spring along the edge of a slough. In a couple of years, my father dug a well about ten- or fifteen-feet deep, and the water was excellent.

William Pitts and Coutts Majorbanks came to the area shortly after we did. Everybody tried to get to work for one of these two men, because they did not have to work too hard. These men were there to have fun. There was much drinking, gambling, and wild parties at their ranches. Coutts Majorbanks was Lord Thursby, a very hard drinker who was shipped out to Dakota to get him away from the family so he would not disgrace the titled English family. He had hounds for fox hunting, but there were no fox, and he couldn't catch the coyotes, although he tried. One day he became angry at his hounds because they were so useless that he went out and killed them all.

There were many dances in the Towner community, old-time dances with a Norwegian fiddler. Melhouse from Villard used to play for us, particularly for the Holling Dance. I remember the first time I ever danced. It was with Maggie McDonough, who married a McGahan and went to live in Sidney, Montana. Maggie's father had no hands or feet, but he could drive horses and do what a ranchman had to do.

I was sick with spinal meningitis in 1896, and after I got better, I wasn't able to ride the range. I tried teaching, but only two of the children could speak English; the rest spoke Norwegian. By the end of the term, the only one I taught, I learned as much Norwegian as I taught them English.

We used to play poker, break colts, swim, fish, and hunt for recreation. For a time I joined the Good Templar Lodge, and I was chaplain, but I joined more for the girls than because I wanted to belong to the lodge.

I remember the vigilantes, a group hired by the Montana Stockmen's Association. They weren't always scrupulous about doing their duty or the method in which they did it. They used to hang anybody they felt like hanging.

Fourth of July celebration at Inkster, North Dakota in 1894

from the Fred Hultstrand History in Pictures Collection, NDIRS-NDSU, Fargo

One summer when I was about six, I had an encounter with the vigilantes. My father was away. The practice then was that anyone who was in the neighborhood ate at the closest ranch. On this particular evening, there were several other cowmen present, among them a half-breed by the name of Gardappi and another who was called Red Dog. Because there were so many extra people, I had to wait for the second table for my supper.

As I waited for my turn to eat, I played outside. I saw a couple of riders approach on horseback. The beauty of the silver saddles and bridles made me forget all else, so I didn't warn those inside of the riders coming. I knew they were vigilantes, even though I was only six. If I had warned them, Gardappi might have hid and been saved.

The vigilantes seemed to know Gardappi. They entered the house and took him. As was their custom, they ordered the rest of the group about — telling them where to stand and what to do — possibly for their own protection so they would not be "pushed." I remember that Red Dog wore a cap of deer skin that still had the horns on it. I still smile when I think of how queer Red Dog looked when he walked to the place the vigilantes told him to go.

The vigilantes made their camp down near Hackett's Ford, and after they took Gardappi away, my mother went down to intercede for him. She couldn't do anything, and he was never heard of again.

I remember the first trap I ever had — I was about seven or eight years old. My father had been to town, and when he returned, he said to us boys with his hands held behind his back, "Guess what I have for you." It was a trap for each of us. I was so excited that I went out at once and set it in a rabbit run. I took a lantern to light my way. The next morning I hurried out to see my trap, and I found a mink. I was too excited to reset the trap. I ran home with my mink to skin it. I did it myself, then turned the skin inside out, scraped off the fat, and put it on a frame to dry.

I also hunted antelope, deer and coyotes. I picked buffalo bones north of White Earth and as far north as Canada. The country was just spotted with bones, and I netted about $12 a ton. The same year I picked bones, Lord Thursby gave a scholarship for the best scholar in the county. My teacher wanted to coach me for that scholarship, but I wanted to go after buffalo bones.

I worked for eleven days building the railroad north from Mandan to Stanton. I drove three horses on a dump wagon at ten cents an hour, and I worked ten hours a day. The wind seemed to blow all the time, and I had a balky team. When I drew my pay at the end of eleven days, I played draw poker. I won $112 that night, and I left camp.

There was a blizzard one year that scattered the cattle all the way to Harvey. There were many prairie fires. I was working on the Eaton Ranch when one of them started. We smelled smoke one day, and one of the men said, "That fire is coming, and we better get ready for it." We got barrels of water and drove to the top of the hill, and there it was! We worked until we couldn't breathe, but we kept the fire from getting into the timber. That was about 1900. I remember that after the fire was out, we lay on the ground and panted for an hour.

The whooping cough and measles came back home about the same time. First the children got the whooping cough, then they took the measles, and five of my brothers and sisters died from it. The year before, my brother, Tim, died of diphtheria.

From England to McKenzie County in the 1890s

Thomas Jefferson

In September 1900 we had about the worst blizzard I know of. . . . After the storm abated we found that there were only three of the 300 head of cattle left.

The son of a Yorkshire, England blacksmith, born in 1863, Thomas Jefferson went to school for five years and had to quit because going farther was "too high for the low class of people." He began working on a farm at age twelve and decided he would leave. He received $5.73 for a year's work. After two years, he went to work in a brewery where he earned $2.50 a day for ten hours work. He went on to work in a steel works where he worked overtime for double pay and saved enough money to go to Canada where he arrived in 1891. He worked on a canal and then for the railroad as a cook. He came to Williston in the mid 1890s.

WHILE WORKING FOR THE RAILROAD I met a man whose name was George Washington. As my name was Thomas Jefferson it seemed odd that we should meet and have so much in common. We had a lot of fun about our names. Our friendship continued until we came to Williston, North Dakota where we parted, and I never saw him again. I arrived on July 3, 1896 with the intention of going on to Montana to find a location.

Williston at that time was not much of a town, but the business houses that were operating there surely did a good business. There was about one block of business places of which eleven were saloons, and each one did a land-office business. I believe the people did more drinking then than they do at the present time. Whiskey was the only thing sold as it was less bulky and as it was against the law; the federal men would visit, and the business places would have to hide the whiskey.

The sheriff seemed to be the biggest horse thief around there so if you got into trouble you had very little chance of any cooperation from him but had to take the law in your own hands. The second day I arrived in Williston Mr. Hedricks who owned a livery stable and a small ranch asked me to work for him in the livery stable and also to take care of the 300 head of cattle he had. When I was not busy at the livery stable I worked on the ranch. After five years of working for Mr. Hedricks I decided to file on a quarter of land.

Mr. Hedricks decided to bring in some Angus cattle to replace the well known Whiteface which were the only kind of cattle seen at that time. He bought 300 head of purebred Black Angus and had them shipped in from western Montana. The cattle cost him $100 each. This was in 1900. That September we had about the worst blizzard I know of, and the cattle were ranging on the prairie when the blizzard was raging its worst. After the storm had abated we found that there were only three of the 300 head left. The others had mired down in a creek. This was a terrible loss, but he bought some more. I was on his ranch in the bad winters of 1896-97, and when I would bring the milk in from the barn, many times it would be partly frozen.

These cattle that were lost in the blizzard were pulled from the creek by the Indians who took them to their camp and ate them. When the Long X lost all its cattle the Indians also cleaned them up for the ranch. The Indians from Fort Peck Reservation would visit the Indians on the Berthold Reservation. When they visited the towns, they would do almost anything to obtain a horse. It seemed that the more horses they brought, the richer they would be. They liked to show off, and after they came back most any pocket knife or ring would a buy a horse from them. It seemed the larger number of horses they could show to their cousins the more important they were in their eyes.

Horses were stolen more than cattle as they were easier to get out of the country. I had a team of identical horses. One day when I went to drive them into the barn, I could not find one. I looked around the pasture and later advertised the fact that I had a horse stolen from me. I finally gave up the idea of ever seeing him again and went in quest of finding another horse to match the one I had left. I heard of a man who had a horse who would be a good match to mine. I called on him, and to my amazement, found the one I had lost. I told him the horse was mine, and he said that he had found him wandering in the pasture without any brand and had caught him and used him.

Another time we lost 15 head of horses shortly after bringing them from Canada. They were stolen in a storm. We were suspicious of the sheriff; we thought he was the thief. Mr. Chappel who was a rancher in Montana was also a horse thief. He would locate a nice bunch of horses and send one of his hired hands to bring them to his ranch, telling the man he had bought them. He sent my friend to get a bunch of horses one time. My friend was caught and sentenced to serve five years in the penitentiary. My friend swore he would kill Mr. Chappel when he got out. Mr. Chappel was found dead not long after my friend got out, but no one connected him to the killing because he left for the Klondike.

In 1901 I filed for a homestead south of Charbonneau, and I bought 50 head of cattle from Hedricks to start with. I was located in the center of two large ranches — Charlie Converse on the east and Franklin Martel on the west. Mr. Converse bought out the Long X, and Mr. Martel became one of the biggest in McKenzie County later. One would think that I would be very unwelcome between these two large ranches; but, on the contrary, we got along fine and never had any trouble. In fact, whenever I went any place, I could get either one to look after my cattle until I returned.

I guess I was not cut out for being a rancher, so I sold out and went to Schafer in 1904 and started a livery stable with another man. We built the barn from lumber we hauled from Williston on wagons. I stayed there two years and managed to have enough business to keep going.

The stagecoach was running at that time, and the driver always had at least two horses each night. Mr. Pebbles drove the coach from Schafer to the Whitehouse, which was located about 15 miles east of Williston near the Bird Head Ranch where he stopped. From there he went to Williston. He would go one way one day and make the return trip the next. Mr. Pebbles was a gambler, and he would rather do this than any other thing. A night never went by when he was at Schafer that he was not gambling or playing poker of some kind. He would often play all night. When he started out in the morning he would tie the lines up some place on the coach and let the horses go by themselves, as they knew the road as well as he did. At least he always seemed to get to his destination. One time when Mr. Pebbles had a gambling date with someone in Williston he found that he had lost the mail sack. Instead of going back himself, he hired a man to find the sack and bring it to Williston. He would rather play poker.

When the stage first started, a regular coach was used — one drawn by four horses. Buggies were in use then, but Pebbles wanted to impress the settlers who were coming in. He wanted them to realize that this was a western country and was plenty wild. Settlers would ride with him

A Cowboys Call.

"A Cowboy's Call" is the title of a colored card romanticizing the early years on the western range

to Schafer or to Farnem, and he would always put on some act to frighten them. If we knew a party was coming in with him to Schafer, we would put on some act to welcome them. Sometimes we would get a horse that would buck, and when the stage come in sight of the business district, we made him buck and cause a ruckus to impress the settlers. It was also common for us to get four or five men to shoot off their revolvers while riding their horses through the street at full gallop, just for the effect. Mr. Pebbles delighted in coming into town at full gallop just to make it look western.

I stayed at Schafer two years and then sold out to my partner. I went to Alexander and rented a livery stable and hotel. I made very good money here as settlers were coming in then, in 1907 and 1908. We also ran a stage from Alexander to Williston and back. We charged all we thought we could get from the settlers who came out and stayed at my hotel and rented horses and sometimes teams and wagons to try to locate a homestead. But these people generally had very little money. After three years at Alexander, I went traveling until 1917 when I bought a small farm on Lone Beaver Creek.

I attended quite a few dances in Williston, but there were very few women present, and many times we would make a stag party out of it. But most everyone would come to dance, for at that time it was quite an event. They were gala affairs, and most of the people brought box lunches and stayed until morning. We danced old-time — waltz, square dance, polka and schottische. The music consisted of a violin, organ or guitar, and a mouth harp. Rodeos were also a good form of entertainment in the earlier days.

When I first came to the United States the first thing I noticed was the freedom everyone was enjoying. It seemed that everyone had a chance to work at whatever he wanted, and he was able to get ahead. The country changed so much that conditions became like those in the old country. The people were divided into classes as they were in England, and I sure did not like to see this take place.

Hunting, Ranching and Forced to Farm in McKenzie County

T.B. Knight

I could see disaster for the rancher. I thought of what the Indians said about leaving this land right side up or famine would result. But those early crops [of the homesteaders] were good, and famine and hard times were a long way off.

T.B. Knight's father died when he was quite small in his hometown of Preston, Minnesota where he was born in 1862. He says that he read stories of the West and "always thought I'd like to live where the country was rough and wild." He started out as soon as he could for Fargo in 1879, but found the Red River Valley too settled, so he went to South Dakota, Nevada and California. Then he trekked back to western North Dakota the year it became a state in 1889 with no more than a horse, a few blankets, saddle and a rifle.

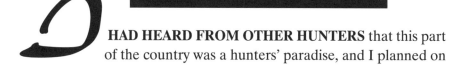

HAD HEARD FROM OTHER HUNTERS that this part of the country was a hunters' paradise, and I planned on hunting for a livelihood. And they were right. At this time, bear, elk, antelope, black- and white-tailed deer, mountain sheep, wolves, coyotes, muskrats, mink and otter were very plentiful. There had been some buffalo, too, but they moved on before I got here. The country was a real wilderness. At that time there were only about twenty or thirty white people living in that vast territory which was later known as McKenzie County.

Indians camped along the Missouri River — all friendly tribes. I traded tobacco and flour for furs they had trapped with a tribe that was orderly and neat. Their chief was Black Eagle. They had well-built log huts along the river, and most of them had a fireplace built in them. In the early 1890s, the soldiers came to put this tribe on the reservation. To keep the Indians from coming back to their homes, the soldiers burned all of their huts.

The country was a great deal different from my home in Minnesota. The river ran in deep valleys. A little way back from the river, there were the flats, heavy with timber. Then came the rough buttes, and after that, the prairie stretched out as far as you could see. The buttes were landmarks with such names as Chimney Butte, Blue Butte, Table Butte, and the Devil's Corner Butte.

The earliest settlers here were all trappers and hunters. By the time I arrived, a lot of ranchers had moved in to what they heard was a great cattle range. At the time I arrived there were several big horse and cattle ranchers. There was the Mule Shoe Bar Ranch established in 1884 by Chase and Frye. By 1889, there was the Long X, owned by the Reynolds Brothers of Texas; Dan Manning's outfit, and Grantier, George Bacon, and the Stroud Ranch. The Reynolds Brothers ran the biggest outfit. With the help of their Texas cowboys they would drive a big herd of cattle from Texas to North Dakota to be fattened each year. When they reached Dakota the cattle would be pretty thin. But the grass here was long and good, so it didn't take long for the cattle to get fat and be ready for the eastern market. The Long X also raised some fine saddle horses.

The big ranchers in those days hired a hunter to shoot wild game and keep the camp supplied with fresh meat. I finally landed a job with Jay Grantier. I kept the outfit stocked with fresh meat. Of course, on a big ranch there were lots of other things to be done, and in the spring and fall every man had to do other jobs. In the spring, there was the branding of calves, and in the fall, the roundup of cattle to be shipped to market. Getting the cattle to the railroad meant late hours and lots of hard work. The big ranchers drove their cattle to Belfield. At the start of roundup the mess wagon with its cooking equipment would go out to a certain place for the noon stop. The cowboys would ride to the farthest point away from the railroad and start back to mess wagon. After the noon dinner we repeated the process in the afternoon. We repeated this day after day in all kinds of weather.

Occasionally, we cut out those cattle that were not fit for market and left them to fatten on the range. Every man took his turn guarding the cattle at night. It wasn't so bad when the weather was nice, but I've sat on a horse when I was wet to the skin and thought I'd freeze. Being out in the open so much, I always had a keen appetite. It always sounded good when the cook hollered, "Come and get it!" The food was always good, and there was always lots of it — nothing fancy: fried beef steak, baking powder biscuits, potatoes, baked beans, some canned vegetables, and black coffee.

A cow camp on the open range

Most of the ranchers had two camps, the home place and a summer camp. Both were located on or near a creek, many of which had peculiar names: Squaw, Horse, Mule, Sand, Charley-Bob, Finnegan, Wannegan, and Tobacco creeks — as well as others I can't remember. Most of these were just little streams most times of the year, but in late spring and after heavy rains they would turn into regular torrents. Then, crossings would be most dangerous.

We didn't do much traveling or visiting. Nothing but trails crossed the prairie, and we had to cross coulees and ford creeks, a dangerous job even in dry weather. We made trips to trading posts where we bought supplies to last up to a year. A rancher would drive his wagon to the river, leave his team at some ranch, go across by boat, walk to town to do his trading, have what he bought back to river, bring it across by boat, and then haul it back to his ranch. He would also bring back all the letters and newspapers — some a year old. The papers would be gone over pretty thoroughly. There were quite a number of small boats along the river. The first big boat which ran commercially was brought in by the James Brothers. Between 1901 and 1905, several ferries began to operate.

There was one ferry near Banks, North Dakota operated by Frank Davis, who later moved down the river near Charleson. Con Sax had one at the mouth of Tobacco Garden Creek. They were cable ferries. The only gasoline power boat was run by Captain Bailey near Williston. In the winter, we made crossings on the ice, but the deep drifting snow and bitter cold made traveling extremely difficult. Some of the ranchers traded at Dickinson, but that was eight miles more distant than Williston, which was 40 or 45 miles away, so Williston became the chief trading post.

A man's credit wasn't questioned in those days. I remember one day I was in the store at Williston when a man came in and bought a year's supply of grub. When he had it all in the wagon, he shouted, "So long, pard!" to the storekeeper. After he drove off, the storekeeper turned to me and asked, "Do you know that man's name?" I told him that I didn't. He put the list and bill on the spindle and said nothing more about it. It must have been a year later that I was in the store and asked the proprietor if he had seen this rancher again. He replied, "Yes, he was in the other day, paid his bill, and bought another year's supply. You know, I should know his name, but I don't. And, gosh, I hate to ask him what it is."

In the summer camps, the doors were never locked. A stranger could always stop at one and find grub and cook a meal, stay over a night or two. If he took anything, the visitor would leave a note telling what it was and saying he would pay for it later. Things were always left neat, with fire wood chopped up for another caller. Nothing was ever stolen. That was the way it was in the days of the ranchers. But, when the farmers began to come here in large numbers, things changed, and not for the better.

What law there was at that time was the law of the frontier. Things ran along smoothly enough, and what little troubles arose were ironed out among the ranchers themselves. Some of the cowboys who came up from Texas toted guns. Outside of them, the only ones who carried guns were hunters and trappers.

I remember one time, a bunch of us were sitting in Sandy Hart's place by the river playing cards, when a man by the name of George Bacon came running in. He had been running cattle for Dan Manning along the river bottom that winter. He asked me if he could use my horse. I asked him what the trouble was. He told me someone from across the river had run off with a steer, and he was going after him. I told him I'd go instead, and I started off. The river was glaze ice and very slippery. My horse was not shod, so it was slow going. By the time I crossed the river, my quarry was out of sight. But I knew who he was, so I rode up to his place. Everything was dark; no one was around. I looked for the steer, but couldn't find it, so I rode up to the shack. A man came to the door and asked what I wanted. I told him. He told me, "You're lucky you didn't get shot last night for snooping around an honest man's place." I told him what I thought of him and what would happen if that steer wasn't returned. He sneered and stalled around a bit and then told me to get off his place and threatened to shoot me if I didn't. I left, and didn't get but halfway between his place and river when I ran across the steer. It had been locked up, and while the man was stalling some of his help had turned it loose.

Some time later, this same man (his name was Shofelt), got into trouble with a man named Dean. One day, a bunch of us were standing in front of a shack across the river when Dean and his little girl drove up. Shofelt was in the bunch, and when he saw Dean, he started to abuse him. Dean was carrying a shotgun in the crook of his arm. At first, he didn't pay any attention to Shofelt's remarks. We all knew that Shofelt carried a gun, and we looked for fireworks to start. After some answers Dean made to Shofelt's questions, Shofelt went for his gun. Before he could draw it out, Dean made a quick turn, and without taking the shotgun out of the crook of his arm, blazed away and sent Shofelt into eternity. Since it happened across the river, a jury trial as held at Williston. There, the jury came in with a decision of self defense, so Dean was acquitted. But these acts of violence were very few. A critter would be lost every now and then, but that was about all the law breaking that was done.

George Bacon had taken squatter's rights on some land on Sand Creek and had built a cabin and some buildings there. He wanted to sell his place, and I had decided to go into ranching on my own. I had worked for Grantier for quite a while, and, when I quit, I took all my pay in horses. The land out here had been surveyed in 1896. In 1898, I moved onto my own place after paying Bacon $200 for the buildings.

But I want to tell you how Jay Grantier got his first cattle before I go any farther. He had been raising horses — and fine horses, too — for some years. One day, we were down at the river on Spanish Point looking around. There was a fine herd of cattle which had been driven down to the shore of the river on the other side. The cowboys were getting ready to drive them into the river and to make them swim across. A man crossed the river in the boat — Miles, the owner of the cattle. Some of Grantier's horses were nearby. Grantier and Miles got to talking about horses and cattle. Miles noticed that Grantier's horses were some of the best in the country. Within a few minutes, a trade was made for a Miles' yearling critter and Grantier' two-year-old horse — and so on. By the time the trading was finished, Grantier was in the cattle business, and Miles went on his way with a fine bunch of horses. Not one cent changed hands.

Another thing — if a man chewed or smoked and happened to run out of tobacco, it was real calamity. Rancher Bill Stroud found himself in this fix one day. He went several days with a terrible grouch on. He finally decided to something about it, so he started for the river and Williston. He got there, and with his pockets full of his favorite chawing, he started back home. But by then, a forest fire had broken out west of us, and by the time he reached this side of the river again, it was smokier than the inside of an Indian teepee. Bill knew that this country was easy to get lost in, but he had lived in it for so many years that he knew it like a book. But the smoke was so thick, he got lost. For several days he wandered around living on his chawing tobacco. He finally stumbled into a squatter's shack, hungry and tired. Now, the squatter was known for the poor food he put on his table and for not being overly clean. But Bill was ready to eat anything. He told the squatter his circumstances. The squatter cooked a meal and told Bill to "set up." Bill ate everything, and when the squatter noticed that he had cleaned his plate, he remarked that Bill must have enjoyed it. But Bill pushed back his chair and said, "A man had to be hungry at least a week before he could enjoy a meal like that."

Anyway, by the time I started ranching in 1898, many new ranchers had sprung up, and the big outfits were beginning to feel crowded. The Long X had suffered a severe blow in the winters of 1896 and 1897, when the snow came early and piled up in deep drifts. Thousands of cattle died. They would drift with the wind and get up against a sharp bank or in a deep coulee, where the snow would cover them up. In the spring, herds were found packed tightly together still standing as they had frozen. Gray wolves and coyotes were hard on cattle too. They would strike at strays, calves, and sick critters. The ranchers always carried guns to kill these filthy pests.

Among the new ranchers to this area were Goodalls and Uhlman. The Uhlmans started the Bird Head Ranch. Charles Shafer was the first man to bring his family to this territory, in 1890. The county seat now stands where he homesteaded. Up until 1900, I don't think there were over eight or ten women in this country.

The summers out here were nice, but a person had to be stoic and hardy to stand the rigors of winter. I always thought there would be plenty of range, but with all of the small ranchers coming in, the range kept getting smaller. The range belonged to the government, but the hay and grazing were free. According to law, a man could cut hay all the way from his place to half way to his neighbor's place. The meadows were better in some places, and the man who had had a good hay meadow had quite an advantage. I had plenty of range and some nice hay meadows, so I was lucky. I continued to do a good business in horses.

But the big ranchers couldn't stand the steady stream of small ranchers that came in. Their big herds took lots of range and hay. The small rancher with his small herd could find enough range and hay. I remember the last roundup that Manning had. He shipped a solid train-load of cattle to the eastern market. He still had some horses left, but he was selling them as fast as he could. He had about a hundred head of nice mares among the horses, and I would have liked to have them. He told me he wanted $100/head for them. I didn't have the money to invest right then. He said, "Never mind. Just go ahead and pick out as many as you want and pay later." It was quite a temptation, but I didn't take advantage of his offer. Many times I have regretted this, because in the next few years I could have doubled and tripled my money.

But I had good range and hay meadows for my horses, so I prospered. Times were good. In 1901, there was another complete survey of the country, but the task was so difficult, it wasn't completed until 1905. Around the first of 1903, the farmers started coming in. The first ones settled around what is now known as Charleson, about ten miles from my ranch. They came from the railroad across Nisson Flats to the river. Then they crossed on the ferries at Spanish and Half-Breed points. It wasn't long before the best land was taken, and claim shacks dotted the prairie. Some of the immigrants stayed just long enough to prove up, but lots of them built their homes and stayed.

Up until this time, I just held squatter's rights. So I began to think that, if I wanted to stay here, I had better make a claim to what I had, so I filed in 1903. I thought that if all these farmers could make a go of it at farming, so could I. There was a lot of talk about organizing this country into a county in 1903. But the ranchers fought this tooth and nail. When it came to a vote in 1904, the ranchers won out. But in 1905, this part of the country was made part of McKenzie County anyway.

All this time, the farmers kept coming in. As soon as they got settled, they started breaking the land. The newcomers got the best of the land. Those who came later took what was left. Along the river flats, up into the breaks, any place they could set a plow, the farmers went to work. I could see disaster for the rancher. I thought of what the Indians said: leave the land right-side-up or famine will result.

Soon, there was something new on the range, barbed-wire fencing. The farmers weren't going to have their crops and gardens run over by range cattle and horses. Before the stock got used to these new barriers, lots of cattle and horses were "out," and there were many arguments. but the farmers coming in here helped me in my horse trading.

With so many people coming in here, there had to be better communication. A few post offices were built, including Charleson in 1905. Before then, mail was delivered by horseback to the Stroud Ranch, where the people from miles around would get their mail. Little stores and trading posts were established as well — at Ray and Tioga, for example.

Little by little, more land was broken, more crops planted. Crops were good, and prices were high. More machinery was brought in. In 1918, I sold all of my cattle after a veterinarian told me they had septicemia. I received a fairly good price. I was in good shape with my farming going fine, but I've always held that this country should never have been broken up. Cattle is the best source of income out here; wheat is the poorest.

Eight-Hundred Square Miles of Range

Mae Caldwell Moran

We didn't know what a fence was in our country.

> *Born in Chicago in 1871, Mae Caldwell's parents were of Scotch-Welsh ancestry. Her father was a commission merchant who, after three fires, declared bankruptcy in 1882. He decided to go west in search for land that would be suitable for farming and ranching. With the help of a land agent, Caldwell selected a spot nine miles south of Taylor. In May 1883 the rest of the family arrived: Mrs. Caldwell, Mae, brother Jay, Uncle Charles, Aunt Brenda and her four children, and grandma. Mae Caldwell Moran tells the family's ranching story.*

In 1882 shortly after he had the third fire Pa took bankruptcy and started out west. He boarded the train for the west and went as far as Livingston, Montana. He left behind my brother Jay and me until he could find a new location.

There was much talk about the West and the money to be made there, and Pa didn't know whether he would get some backing and start in the commission business or get some land and start farming and ranching. A well-to-do commission merchant from St. Louis was willing to back Pa in a new start. Well, Pa looked the country over around Livingston and didn't see a thing that attracted him there, so he started back to Chicago. He met some fellows on the way who were going to Gladstone, Dakota Territory, and when he got that far, he decided that the country looked good to him. Pa stopped there and met J.S. Cryne who was in the land business. Cryne had land there with the Christian Colony and was busy getting people to stay in the country. He took Pa all over and showed him this place and that, but Pa wasn't satisfied until Cryne took him south of Taylor, where he finally settled about nine miles south which was good for grazing and crops. It's a rolling country and a fine one for stock as far as water, protection, and feed are concerned. Pa had been raised on a farm in Illinois and knew good land when he saw it. So he filed on a homestead close to the land he bought on contract and sent for his mother, my Grandma Caldwell; a widowed sister, Brenda Williams; and Uncle Charles Newton. He wanted them to come and file on homesteads while there were still good ones open.

We arrived May 10, 1883 — Ma, Jay and I, as well as Uncle Charles, Aunt Brenda and four children, and Grandma. The snow and wind were blowing a gale that day and the temperature was just 26 degrees above zero. We wondered what we were getting into, but, as kids, we didn't think it was so bad. The older ones were a sorry sight though, and I heard them wonder why they ever came to this neck of the woods.

Gladstone was hardly anything — just a couple of stores, a saloon, section house and piles of buffalo hides, which were a new thing to us; Jay and I could hardly wait to see a buffalo.

The day we landed we were met at the depot by Pa. He had two yoke of oxen, and we started for our new home. Just at the edge of town we saw two buffalo, and Jay and I thought we really in the wild west. Our home in Chicago had been a nice one with nice surroundings, and here we found we had nothing. We found our new home a typical claim shack — 12- by12-feet and practically nothing in it and plenty of lonely country all around. There wasn't a neighbor within seven miles; the school was seven miles away. Our mother had quite a good education, so she helped Jay and me as much as she could. She was lonesome and not too happy in our new home. Jay went to country school a few months in the year, but I never went a day in my life. I was so sickly when I was a kid. I had infantile paralysis with whooping cough along with it when I was two years old. I've suffered from it all my life.

Dickinson was hardly a town when we came. Gladstone was a better trading town in those days, and we did our trading there and at Taylor. Buffalo bone pickers and buffalo were frequent visitors at our new home. Jay and I wanted to pick bones, but Pa thought we couldn't be spared from working on the place, because he got a bunch of horses and about two hundred head of cattle right away and put Jay and me out to ride. It was all new to us, and we got so tired at first, but after a short time we soon got used to it all. My life from that time on was spent in a saddle, and I hardly ever got in the house except to snatch a bit of food and a few hours of sleep. Sometimes we rode the range and covered 75 to 100 miles a day. Seeing 200 antelope or deer at a time was common, and often buffalo got into our herds and traveled with them.

Brenda Williams, Pa's widowed sister, had four children, so a homestead of free land looked good to her as she had nothing and had to work for a living for herself and her four children. In 1884 Brenda's house caught fire while she was down to the river getting water. She had given the children a slice of bread and had gone three-fourths of a mile to the river. Two of her children, a boy fourteen months and a boy three years old, were burnt up in that fire. Folks all over the country came to offer help, and the children were buried right there on the place.

Pa was a hard worker as well as hard on everyone else, and he expected us to work and do nothing else. As young folks we never had much amusement at home. It was a home of all work and no play. Pa drank a lot, and all the young folks in the country knew about it and understood, so they never came around. Sometimes we would go to a dance or get away to a party in the neighborhood. One time in February of 1887 we went to a dance ten miles north of Gladstone with four boys and one other girl. We hadn't been any place for such a long time and were so anxious to go and have a little fun. Well, about two o'clock in the morning we decided we had better start for home, but when we went out we found a raging blizzard. That was just one of the storms of '87. Eighteen eighty-six and '87 were both terrible winters. Well, that night we started out and wandered all over the prairies. You couldn't see a thing; there was nothing to guide you on your way.

Those days there wasn't a thing in the country to stop you. You see, there were no fences, so you just ran circles around yourself. We ended up at Dickinson at seven in the morning after seeing hazy reflections of light through the storm and going in that direction. We were all about frozen to death, and I was the only one that could speak above a whisper, but we decided that we would take what money we had among us and get a room. We went to the Kidder Hotel, and I asked the fellow at the desk for a room. He looked at us funny-like and said, "Do you want room for seven or seven for a room?" I said, "Well, I want a room for seven to thaw out in, and give it to us quick before we freeze to death!" Well, we got the room and stayed there until one o'clock when we thought we could probably stand it to get home and maybe find the way. That trip was a bad one; it took us five hours to get there — 12 miles. That night when we drew into our place, we were almost frozen again, and we met Pa who was mad enough to kill us, but we were so glad to get in the house that we didn't care a great deal.

In the years '86 and '87 we surely saw some terrible storms. I don't think that this country has ever had anything like them since. Eighteen eighty-six had the worst storm. There wasn't a letup for months. There was sure winter-kill that year. In January there was a blizzard that killed twenty head of our cattle right in the barn. For two days during that storm we couldn't get out of the house to even get to the barn to water the cattle and horses. They just died like flies. Some of the neighbors had heavy losses to stuff they had on the range, but the stuff we had was used to Dakota climate and stood up pretty well except the stuff that was thin and in the barn and sheds.

We ran our stuff on the range as long as we could or until the snows came too bad, and then we ran them into winter camp six miles below our place and one down on Plum Creek. At these places we had stacks of hay with about 100 tons in a stack where the cattle could feed. Every two or three years we had prairie fires take the country. They did a world of damage to feed and grain. I well remember the fire of 1885. It was in September, and fall was just starting in. The country had a lot of grain stacks, and everyone had tons of hay. The grass stood three-feet high every place; in some places it was as high as your neck when you walked through it. That time fire went all over the country west of the Missouri and did a lot of damage to everyone. Miles of country was burned, and since the grass was tall, the fire traveled easily. Lordy, that was terrible! Jay and I were in the thick of it as every family sent some-one to fight fires. Pa killed a steer, tied ropes to each end, and then tied the rope to our saddle horns and had us drag it back and forth through the fire. After that fire, you would not have known I was a white girl. The smoke and fire had burnt right into my skin. It took two months to get it off, before I looked like a white person again. Some of the fire-fighters were overcome, as it was hard to get food to us, and none of us had too much water. I remember that for two days I only had one piece of bread for food, but Jay and I did have a water sack that held out for two days.

Some of the fighters had a barrel of water at the edge of the fires and dipped blankets and dragged them through the fires, but we found that fighting by dragging a half steer was the best way to stop a fire. Pa hauled water from the river and plowed furrows around our shack and managed to save that. A funny thing about that fire was that we had six milk cows out on pickets in the deep grass. The fire burnt their ropes, and they ran out of the country away from the fire. We didn't get them back for two months. Pa went to town every day to see if anyone had heard of them, but no one ever seemed to know anything about them. The storekeeper, E.L. Scholfield, said that he would ask everyone who came into the store. Well, one day when Pa was in the store talking to Scholfield, J.B. Little came in and said that six head of cattle had come to his place the day before, and he wondered who they belonged to. Pa described the ones that he had lost; they turned out to be ours. They were in good shape.

Another funny thing that happened during that fire was that we a had a 200-gallon barrel of kerosene on the hilltop by the house. When the fire started my mother gave it a shove and sent it rolling down the hill. It landed in a buffalo wallow where there was grass that completely covered it. The fire jumped into the grass where the barrel was, and the flames there were 50-feet high, but for some reason the kerosene didn't catch fire. The folks expected a terrible explosion, but the fire passed over and we saw the barrel lying on the blackened prairie.

In 1885 Pa got some two hundred head of yearlings. They weren't anything in particular — just everything and not much of anything. Well, anyway they were just range cattle. He paid nine dollars a head for the yearlings and $15.00 to $16.00 for the older stuff. He always tried to get young stuff and fatten it and sell it young. The wealthy man from St. Louis still backed Pa with the cattle he got. He knew Pa was good with cattle and would keep working to make money. He was right, and Pa kept working until he had around 500 cattle and 400 head of good horses. Our range was from Gladstone pretty near to Glen Ullin [about 40 miles] and as far south as 20 miles.

In 1890 Pa got rid of mixed cattle and got into blooded stuff. He now started in with Aberdeen Angus cattle and built up as pretty a herd as you will ever see. It was in 1890 that he got rid of the oxen and started using horses for ranch work. We hated to see the oxen go, as we were used to working them and they were somewhat pets of Jay and me.

Each fall Pa would sell the steers to the St. Paul market and always went with the shipment. We were always glad when our father went away because it was about the only time in a year we had any rest from hard work. In the fall of 1892 he went to St. Paul with a shipment of cattle and came back with a check for $10,000. He borrowed $150 in St. Paul so that he could come home and show the check around.

We had what ranchers call summer and winter range. In the summer we ran them out on the open range and kept about five cowpunchers on the job all the time. Jay and I rode range all the time, too. At our winter camp we had lots of hay and a few straw sheds to protect the weak stuff from severe weather. Every year we put up from 400 to 500 tons of hay. You could cut hay any place and get a ton put up in no time.

Pa prospered, and as I've said many a time, he always got what he wanted one way or the other. He got a lot of land and purchased every other section from the railroad. Then with his homestead and two other sections he purchased on contract he had a good layout and a good place to make money. He also had the homesteads of Aunt Brenda, Uncle Charles Newton and Grandma Caldwell.

In the summer of 1887 there were a lot of rattlesnakes in the country. One day as we rode along we ran right into a den of them. My horse was afraid of them and jumped to the side, but the horse that Jay rode stepped right on one and was poisoned by a bite from the snake. We killed five that day, but there were several more that we missed. Rattlers were quite common in those days, and a bite on horses or cattle sure meant death to whatever was bitten. It was nothing to see a cinnamon bear in a herd. They never did much harm and would walk along with a herd. There were several around when we first came to these parts. Maybe you would call them brown bear, but we always called them cinnamon bear. We liked to see them in a herd, but they were a good thing to keep away from because we didn't know just what would happen if we fooled around with them.

Our ranch was known as the Caldwell Ranch, known far and near. Our brand was the cup and saucer and went something like this ⊔/.

There were plenty of cattle rustlers, and we missed good steers pretty often. The worst of the rustlers that we knew were neighbors. Lordy, those people! They are rich folks now. They were really bear cats.

We didn't have a foreman. Pa did all the bossing. Our mother did most of the cooking at the home ranch, and then at roundup time the cowboys made coffee, cooked beef and potatoes on open fires and used a grub wagon. The grub wagon was used too when it was fire-fighting time, but other times we rode and rode without meals a good many days, except a bit early morning and then a lunch late at night.

I could stand a lot of cold and could ride out in 40-below weather and never feel it, but the rest of the folks couldn't go out without freezing toes and fingers. We don't have the cold weather that we had in the 80s. Nothing like it. In those early days it seemed when winter started it got down to 40-below early in the fall and stayed there, and I've know it to get down to 60-below.

There weren't any neighbors for six or seven years after we settled in the country. There were lots of Indians, but they were friendly, and we liked them. Those Indians and the fellows that worked for us and the folks at home were about all the folks we saw from end of one year till the next.

Max Bloom was one of our earliest neighbors, and one of the best in the world. A.B. Robinson, who came with the Christian Colony to Gladstone, started a drugstore and had a truck farm near us. It was sort of a hobby for him, and he used to walk the four miles to Gladstone and back every day. He often stopped at our place. In the 90s a few Norwegians and Danes came into our settlement.

Branding at the ranch was always done on the open prairie. It was done by roping the critter, throwing him and using hot irons. We never did it any different. In 1896 I had 57 head of cattle, and Pa asked me what I wanted them branded. I said I wanted them branded on the opposite shoulder from his and to use the same brand as his. Well, by '97 the brand was all gone as he just gave them a hair brand in '96. Well Pa claimed that my cattle all got away. I never could believe that, and I always felt that those years of hard work and toil on the Caldwell Ranch were years of the hardest work a woman could do in North Dakota.

There weren't any sheep men in the early days, so they didn't bother us. That is, there weren't any in our neighborhood. War didn't affect our ranch business. Pa could always get all the money he wanted to run on, and he continued ranching till 1917.

We didn't know what a fence was in our country until 1900. Lordy! We had trouble with wire cutters. One time Pa and I followed a fellow that cut wire on the place, and we had to go after him for 26 miles before we got him. Pa and I rode back of him and made him come, and Pa stood over him with a six-shooter until he fixed the fence. To go back to that storm of 1886, I should have said that it lasted from December 13 to April 1, 1887, and we made trips to Gladstone for provisions with a stoneboat and one ox on the river. Folks nowadays don't know the meaning of pioneer days and the struggles we had.

I've been married twice and had a family of three children. My mother and father were murdered in 1917 by a hired man, and brother Jay has passed on, too. In 1917 when Pa died, he was a well-to-do man, but after the lawyers, bankers and the like got to settling it up, there was little left. W.L. Richards, rancher on the big Missouri, bought 200 of the best stuff at the sale. He was one of the finest people I have ever dealt with.

First Lady of the Badlands

Margaret Barr Roberts

It was hard work, but life at the edge of civilization was bound to be hard.

Margaret Roberts, often referred to as the "First Lady of the Badlands," was born in northern Ireland in 1854, the fourth oldest of eleven children. The Barrs came to the United States in 1860 and settled on a farm in Iowa. Jon Lloyd Roberts, whom Margaret married in 1870, was a native of Wales where his father was a minister. Trouble between the son and father led to the son's emigration to America in 1870. The couple moved to Minneapolis where Lloyd was a butcher and cattle buyer. About 1876 Lloyd took a job as meat supplier for Fort Lincoln; she and the children joined him in 1877. In 1881 he became foreman of the large Custer Trail Ranch and two years later squatted on land that was located near Theodore Roosevelt's Maltese Cross Ranch. In 1886 Lloyd Roberts disappeared while he was in Wyoming, and Margaret raised her five daughters on her Badlands place. She remained in and around Medora until 1907 when she moved to Dickinson. During those years she ranched, raised her children, helped out as an undertaker, made loans to cowboys, ran a rooming house — and knew Theodore Roosevelt very well. She was extremely proud of that friendship.

I **HAD A LOG CABIN** three miles south of the Chimney Butte Ranch up the Little Missouri where I was living with my husband and children, and one day in the fall, riding south for a buffalo hunt with Joe Ferris, he [Theodore Roosevelt] stopped there.

Margaret Barr Roberts and some friends in the Badlands
Mrs. Roberts is the lady in white, fourth from the right

Joe Ferris comes to the door and says, "Good morning, Mrs. Roberts, come out here and shake hands with Mr. Theodore Roosevelt."

I came out and there he was, a mighty fine-looking man as I remember, straight and slim with big glasses which made him look queer at first until you got used to them. He was very pleasant-spoken, and after that he used to stop in to see me every time he rode by on the way to or from his hunts. I was told that he had come out for his health, but he never looked sick to me. He was always full of fun and lip, and except for his glasses, no different from the other boys. He was just one of us.

We were neighbors, close neighbors. He lived with Sylvane Ferris and Joe Ferris and William Merrifield at Chimney Butte Ranch, which we used to call the Maltese Cross after the brand of their cattle, and the three miles that lay between our ranches was just a step across the dooryard in those days, to us who used to call 25 or 30 miles just a short distance between neighbors.

Life was rough and simple and hard in those days in the Badlands. There were no comforts, and now and then even the necessities were scarce and hard to get. My husband, Lloyd Roberts, was foreman for the Custer Trail Ranch owned by two brothers, Howard and Allen Eaton. The first year we lived at Eatons'. Then one day I was riding four or five miles up the river and came to a place that I particularly liked.

"I believe I'd like to have my home here," I said.

My husband was agreeable, so in 1883 we built the house in which I lived with my children for over twenty years, all in all. It was a long one-story affair, built of cottonwood logs floated down the river — the same shipment from which Merrifield and the Ferris boys built the original log house at the Maltese Cross. It wasn't a palace, but we had a dining-room and two or three bedrooms and managed to be pretty comfortable as we counted comforts in those days. The roof was just loose logs covered a foot deep with dirt.

I planted sunflowers there, and Mr. Roosevelt and the other boys used to marvel, riding along and seeing the roof of Margaret Roberts' house just one mass of sunflowers, coming up, it seemed, from nowhere. They said it looked funny to see those sunflowers all over the top of a house, and they didn't see how I ever made them grow. I made a lot of things grow those days. I had a garden that was really a garden; in spite of sun and drought, I had it. Every night through the summer I used to draw water, sometimes as much as 20 barrels, to water it.

It was hard work, but life at the edge of civilization was bound to be hard. I'd have been a fool if I'd expected it to be anything else; and I wasn't a fool. I thought it was hard enough while I had a husband to support me, but I wasn't long in the country before I lost him; and it was harder then. He went to Kansas City with some cattle that the Eatons were shipping to market, and he never came back. I had a letter from him from Cheyenne, and that was all. I never heard a word from him again or saw him. He had a good deal of money with him at the time, and I've always said that he met with foul play.

All the burden of the ranch and the bringing up of five little girls came on my shoulders. It wasn't so heavy a burden as anyone who didn't know the frontier might think. There was a wonderful friendliness in the Badlands. No one would think of riding by a ranch without stopping. Cowboys would pull in their horses at all hours and stop for a bit of jaw with Mrs. Roberts and though I wasn't the talker then that I am now, I'd manage to pass the time of day with them. They were good boys all of them, though of course it was the Cross outfit that I liked best, perhaps because I knew them best, Sylvane and Joe Ferris, Merrifield, and Theodore Roosevelt. We were all of us youngsters — I was only at the end of my twenties in those days, and I was the oldest of the lot.

One of the first times Mr. Roosevelt came to see me, he came with Mr. Merrifield. I had just finished churning, and I offered them a glass of the buttermilk. Mr. Roosevelt drank it and thanked me with that hearty, enthusiastic way of his that made you feel as though you had given him a bag of diamonds.

He used to come in often, alone or with the other boys, and we'd visit and have fun all together as young folks will. He was as lively as a cricket and I'd enjoy every minute that he was there. I was full of the old Nick myself in those days, always ready for a joke. When he first came out, he was sad and quiet for his wife had just died, but he was always interesting and friendly and courteous, and later when he got his health and spirits back, he would laugh and joke with the men to beat them all.

After my husband went and I was left a widow with five children to raise and no money to raise them with, the cowboys, and especially the Maltese Cross outfit, sort of adopted me, keeping an eye on me and my children and seeing that we never lacked. I had my garden and some cows and chickens, and we got along comfortably enough. It was hard work but there was plenty of freedom; and it was freedom that I had come west for. There were no such things as fences in those days. Nobody owned land. You would have been insulted if anybody offered you a piece of land as a gift. You didn't want a piece. You felt that you owned all there was.

We had good times. Most of the neighbors, scattered 50 miles north and south along the river, were young, adventurous, simple people. There were a few that were different, but we didn't pay much attention to them. There was the Marquis de Mores and his wife who built a grand house of sixteen rooms near Little Missouri — they were different. They tried to bring France to Dakota, and it didn't work. Then there were some gun-fighters who used to shoot up the town — they were different, but they never bothered me. Then there was Deacon Cummins and his wife. They were different, and they bothered me a lot. They got me mad.

I don't know whether Deacon Cummins ever really was a deacon or not, but he acted as though he ought to be, and he got the name. He was from Pittsburgh, Pennsylvania, and he thought he could make money cattle raising and bought title to a cabin and corral up in Tepee Bottom, two miles south of me; he got a few horses and mules and cows and settled down. His wife came with him. Not counting the women that hung about the saloons in Little Missouri, she must have been about the fourth woman to come to the Badlands.

She wasn't like the other three of us who were just hard working folks with tempers that got out of hand now and then, plain as a cow's tail, without tomfoolery or frills. Not a bit of it. She had been a school-teacher in the East, and she wanted everything in the Badlands just as she'd had it at home.

She was one of those refined women who didn't want to have any work done on a Sunday. She said Sunday should not be made a day of pleasure but of worship. The poor old Deacon had nothing to say. She kept him home Sundays, watching like a dog at a rabbit-hole, seeing that he didn't get out.

I remember once we all rode up to the Cumminses on a Sunday, fifteen of us there must have been and Roosevelt was along. The poor old Deacon, he spoke to us all nicely, but Mrs. Cummins, she was standoffish. Roosevelt was always courteous and gentlemanly, and he asked her in his polite way how she liked the country.

"I like the country very much," said Mrs. Cummins, "but I don't like the people in it. They're rough. They run religion right into the ground."

I suppose she thought that Mr. Roosevelt, being an Easterner and a wealthy man, would sympathize with her views. But he just said, "In what ways?"

"I don't approve of people riding around and making Sunday a day of pleasure," she said.

That took us all down considerably, and we didn't have much use for Mrs. Cummins after that, and Mr. Roosevelt had no more use for her than the rest of us. But she was one of those fool women who want to reform the earth, and just because we knew what she was out for, we made up our minds that she wasn't going to get away with it. I guess God liked our idea of Sunday better than he liked hers for things came about in such a way that we turned the tables on her good and plenty.

One Sunday the boys from the Maltese Cross — Roosevelt and the Ferrises — and Merrifield — rode up to my cabin and said, "Come along, Mrs. Roberts. We're going up to Deacon Cummins' just for the fun of it. We haven't desecrated Mrs. Cummins' Sabbath for so long, she'll think we've reformed."

I said, "Boys, I'm with you."

It was just a matter of two miles or so to Mr. Cummins' and a merrier party of Sabbath breakers you never saw than we were, all in our Sunday-go-to-meeting clothes, when we rode into the Cumminses' yard. We thought the Deacon and his lady would be reading prayerbooks, but they weren't. The Deacon was out in the garden hoeing potatoes, and the Deacon's wife was doing her weekly jobs, baking, cleaning house and making the dust fly.

"Mrs. Cummins," I says, pretending to be shocked, "don't you know this is Sunday?"

"This isn't Sunday," says she, "this is Saturday."

"'Well," I says, "I tell you this is Sunday."

She looked at the boys, all dressed up and shaved, and a more surprised and humiliated woman you never saw. She called to the Deacon and made him come out of the garden; she wouldn't let him finish planting the potatoes.

"To think that I should let myself be influenced so sorely as to lose track of the days of the week," she said in a kind of wail. She didn't have quite so much to say about breaking the Sabbath after that.

But she kept making a nuisance of herself in other ways. She tried to improve the cowpunchers' parlor manners, and Mr. Roosevelt was in on that. It happened this way. One day she invited the boys from the Maltese Cross, Joe and Sylvane and Merrifield and Mr. Roosevelt, to dinner so they got slicked up and went. It was in the summer and naturally they were all in their shirt sleeves for nobody thought of wearing their coats in the summer time. That was a part of the western freedom.

When dinner was ready, the boys all came in just as they were. Mrs. Cummins says, "Well! I notice that you men have not got your coats on," and, of all things, went and hunted up some old coats of the Deacon's. She got one for Joe and for Sylvane and one for Merrifield and one for Mr. Roosevelt. The Deacon's best coat was not too fine, and his extras were a pretty dilapidated looking lot.

Theodore
Roosevelt
in the
Badlands

They were all pretty sore. They were too polite to show it, however, and they made a joke of it. But when they went away, Mr. Roosevelt spoke up and said in his best manner, "Mrs. Cummins, the next time I come, I'll wear my dress suit," which meant that he'd never come again; and he never did.

Mr. Roosevelt was an Easterner; but no one would have known it. He slipped right into the western life like the men who didn't have education but just strong arms and a head full of common sense. His education didn't set him apart. Almost all the other Easterners were like Mrs. Cummins, educated, but at bottom just plain ordinary fools. I never saw such a bunch of educated fools as we got out there from the East in the early days. I really felt sorry for them. Maybe they did know something about books — we didn't claim to know much about those things out here.

My own eastern folks, back Iowa-way, used to think I was going around like a gunman, but I never carried a pistol anywhere that I remember, and I only fired a rifle at a living thing once in my life.

It happened this way. I used to keep a bunch of sheep, fifteen or twenty of them for family use, I having five healthy children that were like to eat their heads off and meat being none too cheap even there where it growed, you might say, on every hill.

One day it happened that my sheep came running in the yard acting like as if they thought the spooks were after them. And there, sure as I'm a-living, right at their heels were five or six of the finest Mountain sheep that ever I seen. The hired man was out. But I says to myself, "By Jiminy, this is a $50.00 shot." Lots of men in those days would have given $50.00 for a shot at a Mountain ram. What I knew about shooting was about as much as an eastern tenderfoot knows about baking bread in a frying pan. But there were the mountain sheep just about in my front yard, and there was I full of the talk I had heard Mr. Roosevelt get off about climbing around all day just for the sight of one of those sheep. So I got the hired man's gun and did with it what I'd seen him do and pulled the trigger.

Will you believe me, I never even scared them? They went right on grazing decent and orderly. I went into the house, and I hung up the hired man's gun and after that I never shot a living thing again.

Other women thereabout were as good shots as any of the men, and all of them were good riders. I was never slow to take a chance as long as I was single, and even afterwards I used to cross the river when nothing but the horse's head and the saddle with me on it showed above the water, but when I had a string of babies, all five of them girls, and lost my husband, I thought that I was beyond the point when I had any business to take risks.

We were a healthy lot of people out there in the Badlands. I myself haven't had a doctor in 40 years, and I've got every one of my teeth and not a decayed tooth among them. And I raised five children of my own on that ranch in the Badlands, and two grandchildren, not to speak of one or two "strays" no one else seemed to have room for.

There was one in particular. Her mother had run off with another man, a neighboring ranchman, and left her two-year-old child in the dooryard.

"That child has got to have a home," I said.

The father begged me to take her.

"I'll take her if you want," I said. "I've got five of my own, and I guess one more won't kill me. But it's only a log cabin I can give her. You search the country. Try to find a better home for her. If you don't succeed, send her to me."

Two days later he sent her to me, and that's the way I picked up that stray.

I lived altogether 20 years on that ranch until I had raised my children so that they could take care of themselves. I made the ranch give me and my children a living and a bit of money besides, and after a while I did a little business loaning it out. The mortgages I would take would be such as the parties and I could write out together. Neither of us would know anything about writing one so it would stand if the lawyers set their minds to knocking it down. The idea was that nobody could afford to disgrace his name by trying to beat a woman. It was a sound-hearted class of people that risked going out West in those days.

I brought up my own five little girls, my two grandchildren and any "strays" out on my ranch on the Little Missouri, educated them as well as I could, taught them to ride and never to be afraid, and saw them married at last to hard-working, respectable men. Then I sold out and took a homestead outside Medora. I just wanted to get off to one side and have a little garden where I could see the Badlands.

Mr. Roosevelt loved it here; and is it any wonder? There were good people here in his day. There are good people here yet, but the West you see today is far different from the West I lived in.

I didn't see Mr. Roosevelt for many years. Then one day he came down the Northern Pacific on a special train and stopped at Medora, and the man I had given buttermilk to and joked with in the old days, as an Irishwoman will, was president of the United States. I went to the station, keeping in the background, saying to myself, "He won't have time to bother with a plain, hardworking woman like me. He won't remember Margaret Roberts." There was a great crowd there, but he spied me.

"Bring Mrs. Roberts up here," he said.

So they took me up and started to introduce me.

"We don't need any introductions," says the President. Then he turns to the crowd and says, "This is the most wonderful little woman in the Badlands."

I saw him once more. It was years after, ten years, I think, and he was going to stop at the station just for a few minutes to shake hands with old friends. That was in Dickinson after I moved from Medora.

I had told everybody around town that I knew Mr. Roosevelt well, and how he used to come out to my log cabin with the Maltese Cross boys in the old days. I knew there would be an awful mob down at the depot when he came through, and I was wondering how I would be able to see him. And I had to see him because I had had so much to say to everybody about him.

There was a man working in the land office, a nice, respectable man, an old bachelor, and he says to me, "Mrs. Roberts, I will accompany you to the depot and see that you see Mr. Roosevelt."

Well! I had been a widow 33 years, and that's saying something for a woman in this country, and he was a nice, respectable bachelor, and says I to myself, "If the neighbors want to make a joke out of my accepting his company to the depot," says I, "let them make a joke of it, and I'll laugh with them too."

So I went, and when the train pulled in, there were a couple of thousand people down to the depot to meet him, and says I to myself, "There's so many here, what'll I do? He won't have time to think about me."

The crowd was calling for a speech, and says I to myself, "This is the end of me, after telling all these people how well I knew him, he'll not have time to bother with an old woman like myself."

He stood on the platform and raised his hand for the crowd to be quiet, and then he says, "Does anybody here know where Mrs. Roberts is?"

Somebody near me shouts, "Here she is!"

The crowd began calling for a speech. But again he raised his hand for silence. "I've an old friend here that I have to visit with before I make a speech," he said.

I was brought up on the platform of his car, and he shook hands with me, and we talked all about old times. It did seem good to see him again. And that was the last time that I saw him.

Ever Westward to the Land of Sheep and Cattle

The Ross Family

So again, we were off in our covered wagon, bound for a new home.

The Ross family left Scotland in the late 1700s and settled in Ireland. William Ross grew to manhood there, but in 1840 he joined the exodus from the Emerald Isle to America, settling in Philadelphia. The family eventually made its way to Kirksville, Missouri. There in 1872 William Ross married Clara Bassett. The Bassetts were of old New England stock. Shortly after Clara and William were wed, they accompanied William's folks to settle near Minneapolis. Their daughter, Mary E. Ross Coulter, tells the family's story from that point.

O FATHER AND MOTHER, who were both courageous and ambitious, came word of alluring opportunities out in the new land of the Dakotas. So father ventured west to Dakota Territory, squatting on land where the city of Grand Forks now stands. This was in the year 1878. There father built a claim shanty 12 by 14 near the Great Northern right-of-way, for James J. Hill was then making a survey for his railroad.

There on June 2nd, 1879, I, Mary Edna Ross, was born and spent my earliest childhood. Some memories of those early days remain; how, as the work on the railroad progressed, mother allowed us children to stand on a table and look through our one small window to watch our father as he worked along the railroad as section boss. Another time he was running an engine. He was a mechanic and blacksmith, having learned his trade in Missouri. Mother and father were now blessed with three children, their second child, Emlie, having been called by our Heavenly Father, and she was laid to rest at Grand Forks. Mother was a Christian and could say, "Thy will be done." She taught us to sing the songs she loved by the firelight of our stove or the light of the moon which shone through our unblinded windows.

Then one day father moved us to a house belonging to one Captain Griggs. This was during the winter of 1882. The four children in the home gave mother and father lots of responsibility. Then one dark cold night the house burned down, and we barely escaped with our lives. Father soon moved to Turtle River, and on March 14, 1885 another son, Clarence, was born. From there we moved by team to Manvel, where father worked for some time in a sawmill. By now the railroad was building west. Father did not want to lose out letting too many go ahead of him. Again he loaded the family possessions. Among these was a sort of cupboard with screened doors known as a milk safe which mother felt could just as well be left behind, as she did not think there would be cows in the region where they were going. Father argued the safe might come in handy, and he had his way.

Father had heard of Devils Lake and had received a newspaper printed at Villard, Dakota Territory, and thither he was bound. We arrived at Villard after days and days of travel. While the horses drank from a creek, father walked up the hill where a man stood in the door of a shanty. Seeing him he called, "Hi, sir, how far to Villard?" The man smiled and said, "This is Villard." He continued, "It belongs to me. Bring your family and come over."

So father called back to mother, and she climbed down and with all the little flock walked up to the cabin, there to meet the editor of *The Villard Leader*, whose name was R. H. Copeland. He advised father to continue on to Minot, so we camped there that night and moved on the next day. It was very hot weather, and trouble was forthcoming, for one of our horses took sick and died. Very well I remember that mother shed a few tears. Father asked her if she wanted to go back home, but she only shook her head and said, "Let's rest here a while." So a small tent was pitched on a lake shore. It was while we were there that some discouraged folks who were headed east came upon us and, as father always said, we "struck up an acquaintance." While they had no horses to trade, they did have an old ox, well broke to work with a horse. Then and there did the milk safe prove its worth. These folks wanted the milk safe, and father wanted the ox, so the trade was made, and we were on our way again. A day or two farther on we came upon some settlers with some ponies. They were not "broke" to drive, but they wanted father's ox, and offered him a pony, and so another trade was made.

In those days a good many teams were freighting between Minot and Bismarck. One of them met us, and in talking to the driver, father learned that they were badly in need of a blacksmith at Minot. So then and there he left mother with the covered wagon and family and rode one of the horses to Minot, telling us he would send someone to bring us in. This, of course, took a day or two. As if it were yesterday, I recall just how the man looked as he rode up to our wagon and said, "Mrs. Ross, you must be a brave woman." Mother smiled and agreed with him, and in a day or two we arrived at Minot late at night. I was awakened by mother saying, "Wake up, dear, and see your father. He is shoeing horses." Just at the same moment I got the smell of food, for someone was cooking supper for us, using the same fire at which father worked while he was shoeing the horses. A lean-to had already been built on the side of this shop. It was of boards, inches-thick lumber, and covered with tar paper. The next morning a floor was laid and we moved in. No sooner was this accomplished than mother was called on by some railroad overseer who came to ask her if she would bake bread to help feed the men then at work on the railroad. So two large sheet iron stoves were moved in, and mother began the task of baking night and day I remember she used the bottom half of two flour barrels for mixing pans. This she continued to do until one May morning in 1887 when a little daughter was born to her. While mother was still confined to her bed, Minot had its first fire, and it was a serious one for it burned almost every small business house along the street. By this time father had been appointed to the office of sheriff and moved the family into a more substantial frame building. A heavy post had been put through the floor into the ground in the center of this one-room building. It served a double purpose, for while it supported the roof at the same time it was used as a hitching-post for such prisoners as were of a desperate type. Here they would be chained both hand and foot. At night father went to bed with them chained to himself, for as yet Minot had no jail. When friends asked mother if she wasn't afraid, she would say, "Oh, no, men have lots of respect for little children." The Indians at that time were not to be trusted, and while they were the cause of many anxious days and nights, no harm ever came to us from them. They were always allowed to take what food they wanted whenever they came. Mother felt the Indians were quite considerate because they took only about one-half of whatever food they found. For instance, if there were two loaves of bread, they took one and with gestures explained, "One for you, and one for me."

Log cabin of kind the Rosses moved to on the Mitchell Ranch

Father soon tired of Minot as a home. The stockmen were now gaining way, and he was induced to take charge of a large band of sheep some thirty-five miles southeast of Minot out yonder in the region of what is now Velva. So again we were off in our covered wagon, bound for a new home, this time in a log cabin on the Mitchell Ranch. It was a bitter cold winter, and feed and water were scarce. The sheep died by the hundreds, and by spring father had had enough of the sheep business. However, some stockmen living along the Mouse River persuaded him to take some five hundred head of cattle to a summer camp at some distance in order to save the hay and feed along the river for the winter time. So again we were on our way. This time a wagon load of lumber with which to build a house accompanied us. Father and my brothers drove the cattle. It was only a two-day trip to the new location known as Cottonwood Lake, about seven miles north of Dogden. In the lake there was quite a large island. Father conceived the idea of building our shanty home on the island. Thus we would have protection from the cattle in case there should be a stampede. It proved to be a beautiful home spot, and mother and we children were extremely happy there. On the island there was quite a variety of wild fruit, wild songbirds, and game. We caught some young wild geese, clipped their wings and tamed them. We had a rowboat which we used to cross the lake to a spring for all our drinking water, and on our way could catch fish for dinner. We made pets of the sand hill cranes which followed us about like pet dogs, and usually called us early in the mornings. We were up at daybreak and to bed at dark. A lamp was never lit unless someone became ill during the night, which was seldom indeed. Summer, as mother said, passed all too soon. The bleak cold weather of fall came on. It was time to go the twenty-five miles to winter range at a place known as Pendroy, which, by the way, was the post office at which we had gotten our mail through the summer months. We lived that winter on the bank of the Mouse River in a large one-room house, and we children walked about two miles to school. In 1890 along with the March winds came another little sister. Times were very hard, and father decided he better head back to Minot where he might get work. When we were settled again in Minot, father became ill from a wound he received when shoeing horses and was unable to work until late in the summer. He then went east to earn what he could in the harvest fields for the winter. When harvest was over, he came home suffering great pain all the time. Mother persuaded him to go to Grand Forks for medical aid. There Dr. H.M. Wheeler operated on his limb, and after a time he came home only to suffer much the same as before.

In July 1891 we had the added happiness of another little sister who came to live with us. That autumn father decided we could not live in Minot where there was rent to pay and other expenses of living in town, so he moved us twenty-five miles east of Minot to a log cabin on the bank of the Mouse River. This cabin was large and had two windows, but only a dirt floor. But that made little difference for there was plenty of wood to burn, water to use, and fish and wild game aplenty. Again father took care of sheep belonging to the First National Bank of Minot, and so we lived on. There was a school about one mile from our home which we attended. In this school there was a teacher and about fifteen scholars with five little Rosses making up the number. During the summer of 1892 the Soo Railroad came up the valley past our home. This brought with it lots of excitement and made life more interesting for mother and all of us. About one and a half miles from us a town was started which was named Velva. That fall an epidemic of typhoid fever broke out at Minot, and father went there to help nurse county patients. Mother and we children with a sheepherder were left to care for home and the sheep. Nothing very exciting ever happened in our little household. Mother received lots of letters from her home back east, and sometimes a package would come with some little treat for us all. We children would look forward to these packages so much that we would walk day after day to the post office only to come home disappointed and some days almost frozen. On one of these occasions mother comforted us by telling us not to give up, for there would be a package for us in a few days.

Full well she knew, for on December 5th, 1892 she gave birth to a son who was named Henry Ernest. Oh, what a package of joy, for we were tiring of baby sisters. Our much loved baby brother was about a month old before father ever saw him. Father was very fond of his little ones but inclined to be gruff in his speech. Looking at the new baby boy, he said, "Hey there, soldier, how did you get here!" This of course amused us all. Little did mother or father know then or even dream that in time this son would grow to manhood, and then one day he would enlist in the World War as a soldier with the United States Marine Corps, there to serve and finally on August 28th, 1919 give his life by drowning in the Artibonite River in Haiti where troops had been retained to keep order even after the Armistice was signed. . . . In the meantime two more little sisters had come, and when the youngest was ten days old, mother was called from her earthly home, October 14th, 1897.

Ranching on the Little Beaver

B.F. "Doc" Spry

The Little Beaver was a beautiful stream.

Most people who settled in Dakota came from eastern states, eastern Canadian provinces, or Europe. Not so with "Doc" Spry (b. 1861). His family, originally from Ireland, left Eugene, Oregon, in a covered wagon during the 1890s and journeyed about two-hundred miles a week throughout the Southwest, and into Mexico, and finally to the Black Hills. In 1900 he and his wife Nora established their ranch on the Little Beaver Creek. "Doc" Spry's observations about ranch life in southwestern North Dakota provide a valuable look at the cattleman's last frontier.

ON THE 7TH DAY OF JUNE 1900 I pulled my outfit on to the Little Beaver and went into camp for two weeks while looking up a location. On the average there was 25 miles between ranches, and every rancher considered it his religious duty to discourage any and all newcomers. On the road coming here I camped near a prominent horseman. After supper I called on him, seeking information as to where I might be able to find a desirable location. He was very kind and very talkative and volunteered the information that he was just about the dumbest man that had ever gone out on the open range. Said he had about the poorest ranch in Montana but that about 40 miles north was the finest country that ever laid outdoors and advised me to go there. I thanked him very kindly and went back to my camp, feeling that I had struck a friend indeed.

Three days later while camped for dinner, a prominent cattleman camped or stopped for the noon hour. I engaged him in conversation and finally asked him where he thought I would be able to find a good location. He told me that he had made a big mistake when he located his ranch but that 35 miles north was an ideal cattle country and advised me to go there as there was worlds of hay, grass, wood, and water and that he intended moving there himself the following year. Two more stockmen gave me the same song and dance. It was always the same — 35 miles ahead I would find just the location I was looking for. At that time I was called a nester and was despised accordingly by the rancher as being his worst enemy.

My pocketbook and my time both being limited, I located on the Little Beaver.

A year later a friend told me that the prominent cattleman spoken of above, when he heard of my building up a ranch, told his neighbor, who of course was a rancher, "What do you know about that? That low-down, dodgasted, contemptible nester has settled right in my back yard"; and I was 18 miles away.

I built up my ranch the best I could that summer and managed to get up 40 loads of hay which carried me nicely through the following winter.

In 1906 Bill Smith, Bill Robinson, Frank Ash, and myself journeyed over to Dickinson to file on our land. We employed a lawyer by the name of George Ould to do our work for us. My filing was made first. After the filings had all been made, our lawyer asked why we did not make final proof at the same time as the evidence was all in, and all we would have to do would be to advertise for six weeks and get a deed to our land. We took his advice and filed and proved up all at the same time after a residence of six years on the land.

For the past 23 years [circa 1915], there has been a vacant eighty in my section. Four years ago I made two applications for a filing on the land, but each time my money was returned to me along with a lot of literature that I could not understand. Three years ago my son made two applications for a filing, and each time his money was returned. A year ago I took the matter up with the authorities at Washington, D.C. They informed me that the land was encumbered by all kinds of government reservations and [that I should] petition the department to have the land designated as nonirrigable and fit for pasture only. Then I could file on the eighty as an additional homestead, which I did.

I have just received my filing papers, and I flatter myself that I am not only the first early-day settler to file on land west of Little Missouri River, but also the last.

The winter of 1900 the CY Cattle Company wintered 400 head of cows and calves at the Smith Brothers' ranch. Two of the company men stayed there to feed and look after them. Glen Hanson and W. W. McElfresh, better known as "Scott," at that time stock detectives, were traveling through the country all of the time trying to catch a farmer or some poor nester who was eating company beef. They had very poor success as I never heard of them catching but one man, and he was coaxed to kill a beef by a detective who had to make a showing or lose his job.

The winter of 1900 the boys that fed the cattle at Smith's butchered four beeves and only one of them bore the company's brand. As the beef did not cost them anything, the boys very kindly gave me a quarter of beef each time they butchered. I appreciated this greatly as I was dead broke at that time and was living mostly on wild game.

Bob Moore, an old time Texas cowpuncher, bought the OX cow camp in the spring of 1900 and was living there when I arrived on the Little Beaver. Moore's wife was an English woman, rather strong minded and very decided in her opinions. Late in the fall her sister came over from the old country for a visit. She had not been here very long before the news went to all the cow camps that there was a new girl at the OX Ranch. Abe Owens, another Texas puncher, rode 35 miles over to the OX and asked the young lady to go to a dance at Wibaux. She agreed to go but insisted upon having a chaperon. Owens agreed to find a chaperon and rode 15 miles to a neighboring ranch where he asked the wife of the rancher to act as chaperon. Being fond of dancing and craving a little excitement, she consented. It was agreed that they would be ready the next Thursday morning at four o'clock. For that dance Owens traveled 100 miles on horseback.

Buggies were an unknown quantity here at that time, but spring wagons were plentiful, and Abe engaged a spring wagon and made ready for the trip by driving 50 miles to the rancher's place on Wednesday.

Bright and early Thursday morning they made their start. The sun was just coming up when they picked up the young lady who had been patiently waiting for an hour and a half. The first day they covered 75 miles and stayed all night at the Sheephook ranch twenty miles south of Wibaux. Here the young lady expressed a wish to ride horseback; she thought it was so romantic. The owner of the ranch offered them horses and saddles to go the remaining distance to Wibaux. This young lady had never been on a horse before, and a two mile ride would have been too much for her; with a twenty mile it's a wonder she didn't die.

A cowboy and his lady cross a stream
The photograph is from much later times.

She was unable to get out of bed the next morning after the dance. She had half a dozen saddle sores, in particular on the side of her knees where the skin was all rubbed off, and they were very painful. After the second day infection set in, but the chaperon being an experienced nurse, headed off complications. On the road home Owens made it a point to stop at all of the ranches and went 20 miles out of his way. He was showing off, and time and trouble meant nothing to him. At Nollett's ranch the young lady could not get out of the wagon, and the chaperon suggested that Mr. Owens help the lady to alight. This he did; he picked her up like she was a sack of oats and set her down the same way. She collapsed and fainted dead away. It was more than her sore and bruised body could stand. Owens delivered the young lady safe but far from sound on the evening of the fifth day from the time of starting to the dance, and on the sixth day he took the chaperon home. As near as I could figure it, Owens was nine days and traveled 300 miles to take the romantic girl to a dance.

Two weeks later he came over to see the young lady, but Mrs. Moore ran him off the ranch with a six shooter. It being late at night, Owens came to my place to stay that night and told me of his hard luck. He was a persevering cuss for he married the girl in February.

In 1898 there was not a house or ranch of any kind on the Little Beaver in North Dakota, except the old OX cattle camp which was headquarters of the OX Cattle Company. The only sign of life in the valley was the wild game and the thousands upon thousands of range cattle that roamed the prairies at that time.

The grass along the Little Beaver bottoms was two feet high, and you could cut a fine quality of hay anywhere on the uplands that would make anywhere from 500 to 1,500 pounds to the acre. There was all kinds of wild game in abundance. White-tailed deer in the river bottoms and black-tailed deer and mountain sheep in the breaks and rough land. It was a common sight to see 75 to 100 antelope in a band. Elk horns were plentiful along the river bottom, showing that elk had at one time inhabited this section of North Dakota. Several pairs of fine mountain sheep horns were found by riders in the early days.

The Little Beaver was a beautiful stream. It was heavily timbered by both cottonwood and ash trees. But, sad to relate, the timber was practically all wasted by the early settlers who in their haste to build up their ranches neglected to either peel or hew the house logs, corral poles, and fence posts; consequently most all of the improvements rotted down in from five to ten years, and the timber was a total loss.

Late in December 1898 the Smith boys moved onto the Little Beaver and located at the mouth of Buffalo Creek and started to build up a ranch. They built stables for twelve head of horses while living in a tent and before they built a house to shelter themselves. In February and March in the spring of 1899 they grubbed ninety acres of sagebrush and plowed all of it and put in a crop of wheat, oats, corn, and potatoes and had a bumper crop with a ready market right at their ranch. They also had a half acre of watermelons that were a perfect crop, but they did not have a market for them.

By the middle of June the boys had completed a big irrigating ditch and a sand bar that gave perfect service all through the summer. The sand dam went out late in the fall after a hard rain. In 1900 and again in 1902 they went to heavy expense to make a permanent dam, but each time the dam went out with the first high water. The project was then given up as not being practical. Thus ended the first effort to irrigate by the gravity system along the Little Beaver.

In the spring of 1900 Bill and George Smith put in a crop of 90 acres of small grain and two acres of potatoes. Speaking for myself alone, I did not see a drop of rain from the 28th day of March until the 15th day of August.

The Smith brothers' crop did not even sprout, not even a single grain came up until after that date. The wheat, oats, and millet came up, grew very fast, and made about one half of a crop, but it was not very good hay as the frost caught it on September 15. The potatoes made a full crop of fair sized tubers that did not get ripe. They were soft and mushy and not at all good to eat as they had a very strange flavor.

When I moved onto the Little Beaver in 1900, I flattered myself that I was a hustler and an early riser. Up to that time I had never had any experience with roundups or beef herds.

By the first of November range cattle by the thousands had drifted onto the Little Beaver and literally swamped me. I did not know what to do as I had more than one man could do to hold my little band of 55 head of cattle. As fast as I would drive 300 or 400 head of cattle away from the ranch, another bunch would take their place before I got back home. I was on the go night and day and was riding my horses to death.

On the 6th of November Bob Moore, an old time Texas cow-puncher who owned the old OX cattle ranch came to me and told me that we would have to get rid of those cattle and asked me very pointedly if I was willing to help drive them out of the country. I assured him that I was more than willing and would be ready bright and early the next morning. Wishing to show off a little, I set the alarm at four o'clock as I had a prideful feeling that I wanted to show that old timer that a nester could have some "get up and git" to him. I got up at four, dressed hastily, donned my cap and mittens, and made a break for the woodpile. When I opened my cabin door, the first thing that I saw was Moore just getting off his horse. His first words were, "Are you ready?" The old scamp had done his chores, eaten his breakfast, and ridden five miles all before four o'clock in the morning. We made a very successful drive, taking 2,000 head of cattle 11 miles. I called it a mighty hard day's work as I had to ride bareback.

On the first day of June 1901 I got up with the sun and was very busy chopping some wood when two four-horse teams drove up and asked if they might camp near the house. I told them that they were welcome to camp anywhere they wanted to. The wagons belonged to the spring roundup and had broke camp and driven eight miles before sunup.

Just as I finished eating my breakfast, Joe Bilyeu, the proprietor of the T Cross outfit drove into the yard and asked about the roundup. I could not tell him anything about it. Then he told me that there were five wagons, and that the roundup would be half-mile west of my house.

Bilyeu had come over in a spring wagon and brought his wife along to visit Mrs. Spry. I furnished him a horse, and by the time we got to the roundup there was a thousand head of cattle already gathered, and as far as I could see cattle were coming from every direction. By nine o'clock the cattle were nearly all in. Just at nine o'clock I was somewhat surprised to see half of the men quit work and start across the prairie like a bunch of wild Indians. I was sure mystified until Joe Bilyeu rode up to me and said, "Come on, Doc, let's go to dinner." Just think of it, dinner at nine o'clock in the morning.

After dinner the men went out to work the herd. Some of the old timers estimated that there were 3,000 head of cattle in the roundup. The herd, being so large and unwieldy, was cut into three bunches and thus was very easy to work.

A part of the men cut out the cows with calves to be branded while others cut out strays or cattle that were to be returned to their home range.

Branding a steer

By one o'clock the entire herd had been worked. Some of the men had dug a hole eight feet long and two feet deep at the back, sloping up to the front in which a big fire had been built, and there were at least 50, and maybe more, branding irons in the fire. Ropers then went into the herd, and as fast as they found a calf following a cow, they would then rope the calf and start for the fire with what I thought was unnecessary cruelty. They always came on a gallup. If the calf fell down, they just dragged it up to the fire where two men were waiting who grabbed the calf just any old way just so they got it. The man at the head would throw the rope off while the other man grabbed the calf's hind leg and yelled, "Hot iron," as the roper called the brand on the cow. And in less than two minutes the calf was running back to the herd. It was exciting and very amusing. When an old long-horned cow got on the fight, it was sure funny to see the men trying to catch the calf and running from the old cow at the same time. When the man with the hot iron was branding the calf, the old cow would become frantic at the bawling of her calf and rush to its rescue. The man with the iron would try to stick the hot iron on her nose. If he succeeded in reaching her nose, the pain would cause her to forget her calf for the moment and she would beat it back to the herd.

At four o'clock, the branding having been finished, the men all made a wild dash for the wagon where dinner had been waiting for twenty minutes. After dinner the men all went down to the creek to wash their shirts.

These few samples of early rising was too much for my nerves so I went home and set the alarm for five o'clock, and it has stayed right there for the last thirty-two years.

A roundup outfit consisted of the chuck wagon, the bed wagon, and eight men, the foreman, day wrangler, nighthawk, and cook. And there were usually half a dozen "reps" or men that represented other cattle companies. Each outfit had approximately 125 head of horses, each cowpuncher had eight head of saddle horses in his string.

I call this the last big roundup. There were ten four-horse teams, seventy-five men and approximately 625 horses, all on my homestead at one time.

Frank Stuart, the MC foreman, gave me a big piece of fresh beef which we were very glad to get.

Bob Devine was range boss at that time. He had been to Camp Crook on some important business, and on his way back to the roundup he stopped at the CY pasture at the mouth of the Boxelder to rest for an hour and let his horse graze. After sleeping an hour, he tried to catch his horse. But the horse would not let him catch him. Devine swore up and down that he followed that horse three times around the pasture before he gave up and started to walk to the Nels Rasmussen place on the Little Beaver, a distance of 20 miles. He did not find the wagon as he expected to, so struck out bravely for my place, eight miles farther where he arrived at three o'clock in the afternoon. He ate breakfast in Crook and did not get anything to eat until he caught up with the wagon at my place. He had walked at least 35 miles through the gumbo in high-heeled boots. It took a lot of sand and a lot of grit to make that trip on foot.

Railroading, Then Ranching on the Little Missouri

Alfred White

A fellow in the early days planned on roughing it and didn't expect to have everything just so.

Born in 1857 in Faversham in Kent, England, Alfred White finished the equivalent of high school and went to work at age fourteen. Within a couple of years he was employed on a railroad in England and eventually in Texas and on the Santa Fe in New Mexico. He came to Dakota Territory in 1883 to work on the Northern Pacific. He also went to Alaska and Montreal, Canada, and did "about every job the railroad had." He didn't want to live at either Mandan or Glendive, Montana, so he had to decided to quit the railroad when he was offered the chance to live in Dickinson. He stayed on, and Alfred White was in Medora in the earliest days.

MEDORA AT THIS TIME was only an infant. Soldiers located there on the Little Missouri River. At the west end of the railroad bridge were three small houses and a hotel, and farther down at the south side of the railroad, a section house. The hotel was run by Pete Molloy.

Once, one of Molloy's patrons asked him for a clean towel. He asked the fellow what was wrong with the towel that was there; three or

85

four hundred others had wiped themselves on it and never kicked. It goes without saying that the patron didn't get a clean towel. Later, Molloy had an attack of delirium tremens and was turned over to the first druggist in Medora, who said he could fix him. He did with a shot in the arm that fixed him for good.

On the other side of the street, there was the Pyramid Hotel, run by Frank Moore. It was here that Theodore Roosevelt stayed when he arrived at Little Missouri in 1883. I don't remember seeing him until the town of Medora was started up. One day, Roosevelt was bucked off by the horse he was trying to ride. He broke his glasses. He was more worried about those glasses than any broken bones.

In the early 1880s, people began to realize that this country was a ranch country. Land, land, land — and plenty of it — to range cattle without cost. There was good grass and plenty of water. The first range cattle I remember seeing were owned by Berry Boice Cattle Company, a group of Colorado fellows who brought cattle from Texas. They were brought in by J.W. Follis and turned loose at Keith, about a mile and one-half east of Beaver, now called Wibaux, Montana. Bill stayed with that outfit for 14 years as foreman. It became well known as Three Sevens (777).

Ever since I came to this country, I have been more or less interested in ranching. As early as 1885, just two years after I came, I started in the ranch business. I started out here in McKenzie County on a creek that I named Charlie-Bob Creek. I named it for Charlie Trask and Bob Fuller who had cattle and horses out here in this country. They ran their stuff all over this country.

In 1890 I decided to start up ranching over on the Little Missouri River located on Sand Creek. At the time I bought it, it had only a dugout, small stable, and a corral. But with an unlimited amount of range and good water, I could see that this place had more to it than poor buildings. My nearest neighbor was Mrs. Margaret Roberts who was down the river a few miles. Her husband, the foreman at the Eaton Brothers Ranch, left in 1886 to purchase cattle in Kansas City, Missouri. He never returned. Mrs. Roberts raised here family of five daughters to womanhood alone. She did a good job, too; and everyone in the country admired her courage. Her log house was right in the Badlands. She rode the range and never faltered in the work that was left for her to do. She continued on in the cattle business and gradually got a nice herd together. She sold old stuff each year and saved her money. She became a money loaner to cowboys who wanted to gamble or buy cattle. These cowboys always paid her double, or as high as 12 percent interest for the loans. Charlie and Bill Colgrove started the old Lime Kiln Ranch in '82 northeast of Lefor. That was quite a sheep ranch; they did quite well. But sheep and cattle didn't go together as far as ranching went, but many of the early ranchers had cattle and horses. With the open range, it was an easy matter to have horses, as they needed little care. I'd say that most of the ranchers quit because of open range being lost to homesteaders.

Cowboys in front of a bunk house

Index

Dakota Cowboy & His Horse in Their Finest

Roundup in Western Dakota

Editors D. Jerome Tweton (left)
and Everett C. Albers (right)

*T*HE WAY IT WAS: THE NORTH DAKOTA FRONTIER EXPERI-
ENCE has been a longtime project of editor D. Jerome
Tweton, who spent countless hours of many years reading through the
5,000 interviews of the first settlers of northern Dakota Territory and
then North Dakota done in the 1930s in one of the great public humanities projects of the past, a Works Progress Administration (WPA) project which invited all states to gather the narratives of the oldest pioneers still alive to tell their stories. Tweton invited Everett Albers of the
North Dakota Humanities Council to join him in the early 1990s — the
project has been completed with the publication of the sixth volume
and a boxed set of the six in the series a decade later.

About the editors . . .

Historian D. Jerome Tweton returned to his hometown, Grand Forks, North Dakota, to teach in the University of North Dakota history department in 1965 after receiving his Ph.D. from the University of Oklahoma. For most of his thirty-year tenure at the University, he served as department chairman. Tweton's books include The Marquis de Morès: Dakota Capitalist, French Nationalist *and* The New Deal at the Grassroots: Programs for the People in Otter Tail County, Minnesota. *A senior consultant to the North Dakota state partner of the National Endowment for the Humanities, Tweton has written and edited books and articles about the history of North Dakota for citizens of all ages, including text books and instructional material for classroom use. In addition to his work as an academic historian who has edited publications, written seven books and scores of articles, Tweton has participated in over 300 public humanities programs in North Dakota and throughout the nation. He and his wife Paula own and operate a bed-and-breakfast in a renovated turn-of-the-century home which is on the National Register of Historic Places, the Beiseker Mansion in Fessenden, North Dakota.*

Everett C. Albers has served as the executive director of The North Dakota Humanities Council, the state partner of the National Endowment for the Humanities, since it began in 1973. Albers is one of the founders of the modern Chautauqua movement which features first-person characterizations of historical writers and thinkers presented in tents during summer tours of the Great Plains. He holds an M.A. in English from Colorado State University and has taught humanities and English. A North Dakota native who grew up on a family homestead in Oliver County, Albers lives with his wife Leslie in Bismarck. They are the parents of Albert and Gretchen. Albers operates Otto Design, a desktop publishing concern, and the publishing house Northern Lights, ND Press, as an avocation. He co-edited The Legacy of North Dakota Country Schools *and the 1998* Behold Our New Century: Early 20th Century Visions of America *and has written several children's coloring books featuring Seaman, the dog who went with Lewis and Clark, as well as the 2002* The Saga of Seaman: The Story of the Dog Who Went with Lewis & Clark.